The Child Within

Angela Joy

JOY OF MY HEART

RENÉE ROGERS BANNING

ISBN: 979-8-218-43991-0

Cover illustration and photography by Abigail Newton, granddaughter of Renée Rogers Banning.
Contact at: abbynewt11@gmail.com

Interior design and book packaging by Stephanie Whitlock Dicken.

—∿∿—

To Amy and Andrew, who lived it with me...
And to **every** "Child Within"...

—∿∿—

—m—

The Child Within

is indeed a child

—m—

The Surprise

MARCH 15, 2002

Hello! My name is Angela Joy, and this is my story. I was born 16 years ago today, but I am going to start at the very beginning. I was conceived on October 5, 1985, sort of "accidentally", some would say. But neither my mom nor I think that my conception was an "accident." Let Mom explain further:

3 AM – NOVEMBER 10, 1985

I am more than three weeks overdue…could this really be happening to me? Yesterday I went to Edward's Pharmacy, praying that no one I knew would see what I had just purchased…a home pregnancy test! My usual pharmacy was out of the question; the clerks all knew me there, and I was too ashamed to buy what I am now holding in my hand. The directions say: "For more accurate results, use the first void in the morning." In fearful anticipation of what might be true, I have awakened at 3 AM… surely this must count as "morning". I just cannot wait any longer…

My hands are shaking so badly, I can hardly pee on the test strip, let alone read the results…

What? It's a (+)?! You are kidding me!

"No, Lord! Please, Lord…how could You let this happen to me? I just can't believe this! I know what Harland and I did was wrong, but we used protection. Surely this cannot be!"

I need to talk to someone. Who can I call at 3 in the morning? Immediately my friend Jim in Seattle popped into my head. After hearing a groggy "Hello," I blurt out: "I'm pregnant!" One second of silence seemed to last forever. Finally, I hear: "Renée?"

"Yes, Jim, it's me...I'm pregnant!"

"Are you sure?" I told him I was seeing the evidence with my very own eyes. My test was a (+)!

Trying to reassure me, Jim replied, "Oh, those home tests really aren't accurate, are they?"

I feebly replied, "I'm also more than 3 weeks overdue, and I'm having morning sickness every day."

The truth was, I knew the exact night I got pregnant (with a condom, mind you) because it was the night I went over to my boyfriend's house to tell him I could not go to bed with him because of my convictions as a Christian. If it wasn't so darn pitiful, it might be funny. Temptation and feelings of love and loneliness won over that night, and now I was facing the consequences of my actions.

Harland and I had been dating for about 4 months, and we had slept together one other time, again using protection. I was not on birth control pills because I really was not "sexually active" in my mind, so I thought there was no need. And I really did mean to tell Harland that night that we could not make love again because I knew God said it was a sin outside of marriage. So much for my good intentions...

I will never make an excuse for my actions, but I was a vulnerable woman in a vulnerable place. My first marriage ended in divorce when my husband had an affair with my best friend. I had been a single parent for eight years and was so tired of dating. I wanted to be married, to be cuddled, to be loved, to be cherished. This man seemed like he could be "the one." Not only was he tall, dark, and handsome, he was a great father to his three boys, so I thought he would be a good father to my son and daughter. But I never, ever imagined that I would get pregnant! This was certainly not in my plans.

Jim then woke up his wife, who got on the line with him. Together they talked with me about my options - did I want to keep the baby, or would I consider an abortion? His wife confessed that she had had an abortion; she said it wasn't too bad. But for me, I knew that was not an option. For years I had felt in my heart that abortion was wrong, so now that I was the one pregnant, how could I think it was OK for me to do it?

For me, this was never a "choice."

Angela: "Whew! Was I ever thankful that my mom was familiar with God's Word, the Holy Bible. She remembered reading David's words to God in Psalm 139.

'For You created my inmost being; You knit me together in my mother's womb. I praise You because I am fearfully and wonderfully made; Your works are wonderful. I know that full well. My frame was not hidden from You when I was made in the secret place. When I was woven together in the depths of the earth, Your eyes saw my unformed body. All the days ordained for me were written in Your book before one of them came to be.' Psalm 139:13-16

Mom did not realize it then, but my tiny, rudimentary heart had already been beating for almost a week. The formation of a human is indeed a remarkable process...no wonder people call it a miracle...it is! Every day my body was experiencing new changes, as God was "knitting me together" into human form."

—∞—

Decisions...

Early the next day, after getting my two children, Amy and Andrew, off to school, I had time to really think and pray about what I was going to do. Two things stood out: #1. I needed to tell Harland, my boyfriend. #2. I needed to tell someone who would support my decision NOT to have an abortion. I was not ready to deal with #1 yet. So…what about #2? Who would encourage me to not have an abortion?

First, I thought of my friend Meredith. She and I attended college together, but we did not become close friends until several years later. Meredith is a strong Christian and agrees with me that abortion is wrong. She and her husband were there for me during my painful divorce, and I feel she will support me in my decision to keep my baby. But how embarrassing it will be to have to tell her I am pregnant.

Then I thought of my friend Mary. We attend the same church, and although she and her husband John are in a different Sunday School class because they are older, we are very good friends; I know them well. All four of their children have been babysitters for my kids at one time or another. She and her husband had also been such a big support for my children and me both during and after my divorce. Although they are not old enough to be my parents, sometimes I feel like one of their kids. I really expect that Mary will be there for me as I walk through this pregnancy. I know she will have a lot of wisdom to share with me.

Connie is another close friend who I know will be there for me during this pregnancy. Connie was my neighbor during the rugged days of my divorce, and she was one of the few friends I shared with when my ex first walked out on me. Oh, and she is Catholic, so she will agree with me about not having an abortion. Yes, I think I can tell Connie.

Next, I thought about Dr. John York, an OB/GYN from my church. He had recently led a discussion in my Sunday School class about abortion. He told us he had taken a stand in his medical office practice, and that he did not participate in this procedure. I knew he was the doctor I should go to. But again, I thought of the humiliation I would face because he knew me from church. Once again, my pride in being seen as a "good" Christian caused my hesitation about telling anyone my secret.

Nervously, I make a phone call...

"Meredith? Can I come over? I need to talk to you about something..."

—⁂—

Meredith's reaction was what I had hoped for when I decided she would be someone I could tell about my pregnancy. She was shocked, of course, but very gracious towards me. And I was right about her supporting my decision to not have an abortion. The only problem is that she and Jan are moving East for almost four months, so she will not be here for most of my pregnancy. They will be leaving right before Christmas and won't be back until April. I know she will be available by phone, but I cannot help wishing she would be close enough to give me a hug when I need one. I know there are hard times ahead of me as I face telling people (especially my family) about my pregnancy. I also know there will be times when I am just having a bad day because of these totally unexpected circumstances. Yet, I know Meredith's prayers will be with me, and that is what I need most of all.

"Thank You, Lord, for Meredith's grace towards me. And thank You that I have such a precious friend."

—⁂—

Speaking to Mary was another story - one that took me by surprise. Her first reaction was to jump on me because I got pregnant.

"You are old enough to know how to use proper contraceptives! How could you have let yourself get pregnant? You should know better!"

Not what I expected from Mary. She seemed a little mollified when I told her that we had used a condom. I think she was just shocked, and did not know what to say. In the end, she did encourage me to have the baby, although she was not sure if I should keep the baby. She knew that I had had a lot of financial struggles being a single parent.

That was true for me until I got my nursing degree, but I had learned to live frugally before I became an RN, and I used that knowledge to live well, now that I had a good paying job. I told her I did not think I could carry a baby for 9 months and then give it up. Good grief! I am 38 years old! It is not as though I am a 16-yr old, dependent upon my parents and without an education. I knew that God had provided for me during the tough years after my divorce, and I really believed He would do the same now and in the future.

When I got home, I cried; I felt hurt by what Mary said. Why did she seem to react so harshly about my news? I know I made a wrong decision to sleep with Harland, but we did try to prevent a pregnancy. Will Mary be there for me like I thought she would? I am not so sure anymore. Time will tell…

—⚬—

Next, I called Connie and asked her if I could come over to talk to her about something. She welcomed my visit, but she was definitely surprised when I told her my news. She knew who Harland was, and knew that we had been seeing each other since July. As expected, she was very supportive of my decision to have the baby. She said she would be there for me during this difficult time. She has always been such a blessing in my life.

Now that I have told some of my closest friends, the next hurdle is to make an appointment with Dr. York. Am I ready for this pregnancy to be verified? I am not so sure…

But now I need to make a cake. Andrew turns 9 today and four of his buddies are coming over tonight for pizza, presents, and cake. Focus, Renée…

—⚬—

Confirmation...

NOVEMBER 13, 1985

Today is the day I am going to find out for certain that this is real. I finally called Dr. York's office yesterday to schedule an appointment with him. Of course, they asked me why I wanted to see him. It was so hard for me to say the words: "I think I'm pregnant."

Anyway, they had me stop by their office to pick up a sterile cup so I could give them a sample of my first void the next day. I took the sample in early this morning, and I am awaiting their call.

"Oh, Lord, let me be wrong about this! Please, please, let this all be a mistake."

Angela: "You may think that it is hard for me to know how much Mom wanted me not to be, but who am I to judge her? You will see that God is going to use me to do some mighty things in my mom's life. Our God of love is still in control - even when we humans mistakenly think that we are. Sometimes I wonder if God laughs at our frantic attempts to keep control over our lives. Maybe not, but I am sure He shakes His head a little bit.

By this time, I am about 5½ weeks after conception, and my brain, spinal cord and other tissues of my central nervous system are forming. My heart and liver look large in comparison to the rest of my body. My arms and legs are tiny buds on my torso. Now Mom will continue with her story."

It's real! I just got the call from Dr. York's office. I could not help myself, but I burst into tears as soon as I heard the nurse say, "Congratulations!" She told me they wanted to schedule my first appointment, so I go in to see Dr. York next week. I am dreading having to face him. I have been crying and praying all afternoon, but the kids will be home from school soon. I cannot let them see me this way. I need to wash my face with cold water, and get myself together. And I need to call Harland to set up a time to see him and tell him this devastating news.

—∞—

"Harland, this is Renée…Can I come over tomorrow evening? I really need to talk to you about something."

—∞—

Telling Harland

NOVEMBER 14, 1985

After securing a babysitter for tonight, I am getting ready to head over to Harland's, and I have been praying like mad all afternoon.

"Lord, I need Your help again. I just do not know how I am going to tell him. I know he is going to be as shocked as I was because we did use protection. Condoms - less than 1% failure - how can we be so lucky? And who will ever believe that we had had sex only one other time? I know, I know...even once was wrong...But I don't understand...how could You allow this to happen, God?"

OK, I know it sounds like I am trying to put the blame on God, but I truly believe that He is in control of our lives. But like any good father would do, He allows us to face the consequences of our behavior. I guess I just wanted Him to give me a pass this time.

—◈—

My heart is pounding much, much louder than the quiet little rap I make on Harland's door. Am I hoping he will not hear me, and I can go back home?

Although greeted with a hug and a kiss, my fear is that he will soon tell me to leave. I swallow, take a big breath, and shoot up a quick prayer to heaven. Here goes...

"Harland, I need to tell you something... I am pregnant."

"What?! How could that be? We used protection!"

"I know we did; but I am sorry to say it was confirmed at the doctor's office yesterday. I am almost 6 weeks along. Believe me; I am just as shocked as you are!"

After a moment of stunned silence, he asked me, "So what are you going to do? And what does this mean for you and me, and our relationship?"

I looked him right in the eyes, even though it took all my courage to do so. Then I said, "First of all, you need to know that I am going to have this baby. In my heart I have always believed that abortion is wrong, and I can't change my mind just because I am the one who is pregnant. I simply cannot go that route; I am sorry if you do not agree with me. But I know in my own heart who I am, and I just could not live with myself if I had an abortion. Since I am the only one who must live with myself, I must do what I feel is right.

I know you need some time to think about this. Believe me, I have been as stunned and shaken as I am sure you are right now. I think it best if I go home now and give you some time to absorb this news. We can talk again in a couple of days. As far as what it means for our relationship, only time will tell."

Angela: "Well, now both Mom and Dad know about me. It is obvious they are both still in shock. I don't know if Dad will think Mom did this on purpose so he will marry her, but I can tell you that getting pregnant was the last thing on her mind. The only way to accept this is to believe that God has His purposes in creating me. Meanwhile, my body continues to change by the hour, as God makes me into a perfect little girl. Of course, it is too early for Mom and Dad to know my sex yet."

Fitful First Physician's Physical

NOVEMBER 20, 1985

As I sit here in the OB/GYN waiting room, I immediately look around furtively to see if I know anyone. Or should I say, to see if anyone knows me? It is not like I am wearing a sign that says: **"I'm pregnant! …Not married!"** Why does it feel that way?

Phew! No one knows me. But as I spot so many obviously pregnant women around me, I cannot help but wonder if I am the only one here who wishes they were not. What will Dr. York think of me? What will everyone think of me…? When are they going to call my name? Do they have to say it out loud? Just nod at me. I'll come…

Wow! I had forgotten how many prenatal tests were required when you are pregnant: Hemogram, Antibody Screen, Blood Type, Rh Factor, Rubella - (Yes, I've had the measles – 3 times when I was a kid!), Prenatal Panel, Toxicology Screen. Do I have any blood left? And my personal favorite – peeing in that little, tiny cup! Who can do that?!

Now, here I sit in the exam room…waiting. Most times we are watching the clock, waiting impatiently for the Dr. to come in, but today I am dreading that door opening, fighting off the tears that want to turn into sobs. I feel like I am in the Roman Colosseum, waiting for the gate to lift so the beasts can come in…

OK, so that is a little dramatic…

Finally, Dr. York walks in with a look of "grace" on his face, not condemnation. It was then that the sobs came. His kindness and patience as he allowed me to weep will not ever be forgotten. Once I was calmer, we talked about my options. I told him I came to him because I knew he felt the same way about abortion as I do…that it was not a "choice" for me. He reassured me that he would be there for me in whatever way he could be.

He said, "Everything will be OK, Renée. We will walk through this door together - with the help of the Lord. You can do this. I have seen your strength through other rough times in your life. It is all going to be alright."

Dr. York then talked with me regarding the fact that I was 38 years old. He told me there was a real possibility that I would have a Trisomy 21 baby (previously called "Down's Syndrome"). He told me about a fairly recent test called Chorionic Villi Sampling, often called CVS. He explained that the exchange of placental nutrients and oxygen between the maternal and fetal blood takes place in tiny, finger-like projections called chorionic villi, which are submerged in tissues filled with maternal blood. Wow! That is a mouthful!

He went on, "In each villus, fetal blood circulates through a minute blood vessel, or a capillary. This test takes a very tiny sampling of the villi, which shows the chromosomes of the baby, and then we can see if anything is atypical. You can also determine the sex of the fetus, if you want to know it."

Although I am a nurse, I do not remember learning about chorionic villi, though I probably did. Dr. York explained that CVS can be done earlier in the pregnancy than an amniocentesis, and it is a little less invasive. Also, the results usually come back much quicker. Because this technique was new, he had not been trained on how to do it, and I would have to go to Portland and have it done by another doctor.

Honestly, I did not know what to think. I am just still trying to absorb the fact that I am pregnant. This was not a decision that I could make lightly. I was not ready…and I needed to discuss it with Harland. I told Dr. York I would go home and think about it and let him know. And I really needed to pray about it.

Angela: "I am about 6½ weeks old today. Although my ears are now beginning to develop, it is by God's grace that they are still immature, and I did not have to hear the sound of sobbing as Mom sat in Dr. York's exam room.

Even though my ears are immature, there are many exciting changes going on in my body. Now my blood cells are formed and some circulation begins. You can see my spinal column through my thin skin. My ribs are forming too. The beginnings of my eyes, nose, and mouth are showing; I admit my eyes look a little scary at this point - they look like dark holes. All my organs are formed, although some are still very rudimentary. My arms and legs are growing a little longer each day. My hands and feet are just beginning to show. My fingers are not distinct yet; they are still webbed. They make my hands look like paddles. Ping-pong, anyone?

It is all quite breathtaking! Every day my body is changing, bit by bit - or should I say, cell by cell - as God continues to mold me into the little girl He has planned for me to be."

A Painful Question

NOVEMBER 23, 1985

Harland called and asked me to come over. He wanted to talk more about our situation. After securing a babysitter, I am on my way to his house. My stomach is doing flip-flops as I think about what will happen, and what he might say to me. Will he be angry rather than speechless, as he was on my last visit? Surely he won't think I got pregnant on purpose so that he would marry me. As I approach his house, my heart is about to beat out of my chest. It sounds louder to my ears than my feeble knocks on his door.

—⁂—

Our talk began with the worst thing he could say to me. He asked, "Are you sure this baby is mine?"

That hurt…big time! Does he not know me any better than that? I assured him that since I had not had sex with anyone else, it was most definitely his! It makes me wonder if he shared our news with someone who questioned my motives…and my morals…someone who does not know me. At least Harland seemed to believe me after we talked some more.

Later, we discussed more practical things. He offered to pay for half of the medical costs, which was a great relief to me. I had not even thought that far ahead. I am just trying to get through today. Thank God I have decent insurance at the hospital where I work.

We also agreed to continue to see each other to see how our relationship develops. I told him I would keep him informed of medical appointments, etc. I shared with him about my first doctor's visit on Wednesday, including the possibility of having a CVS done in Portland.

I did my best to explain to him what that was. In my heart, I wondered if he hoped that something would be wrong with the baby so I would lose it. Maybe not, though. I just did not know...

A "Thankful" Thanksgiving?

NOVEMBER 27, 1985

Thanksgiving week...the kids and I are headed to my older brother's home in Hoquiam, Washington. Rodney and his wife Toni are pastoring a small church there. My parents are meeting us at my brother's house, and we are all spending Thanksgiving weekend together. My younger brother and his family were unable to come this time.

Normally, I would be looking forward to this family get-together, as we always have a lot of fun - even to the point of great silliness. But not this time...the closer we get, the more knotted up my stomach is becoming. I am just not ready to tell my family about the baby. They will be so disappointed in me. Plus, I do not want to ruin their Thanksgiving.

The problem about keeping quiet is that I am having a lot of morning sickness already. Basically, I get up...and throw up...every single morning...! So how can I hide this from my family? Have you ever tried to vomit quietly?

Not only that, I know that every time we visit my brother's church, we are a part of Sunday's worship service. Can I really stand up there, knowing that God knows I am pregnant...even if my family does not?

Sure enough, as soon as we got here, Rodney started telling us what we were going to be doing for Sunday's service. He wants me to read the scripture for the day. Then all of us will be singing the "Special Music" together. Oh, great! Just what I was afraid of...

Normally, practicing singing with my family is fun – lots of laughter and joy as we all figure out our parts. Dad plays the piano by ear, and usually we all sing our hearts out. We are not ready for "Prime Time," but we are not too bad… But this time there is at least one heart breaking as we practice our song. I feel like such a hypocrite!

—⁓—

Thank goodness, the weekend is over! Sure enough, I was vomiting every morning before breakfast. I discovered that you can go in to pee, and then vomit right as you flush! It hides the sound of retching. Not only have I had to hide throwing up, on Thanksgiving Day we had to go around the table and tell what we were thankful for. I don't even remember what I said; I just know that I felt deceitful and ashamed. Can you imagine what was going on in my head all weekend?

"You hypocrite… hypocrite… hypocrite…"

It especially resonated when I read the Scripture for Sunday's service and sang with my family. And guess what my brother picked out for the special music: "Amazing Grace." I think God had a hand in that. I think He wants me to know that His grace is sufficient for me. But at times, I wonder…is it?

"Is it, Lord?"

Angela: "My Mom is a little hard on herself, isn't she? She needs to remember that she has a very loving family. Yes, they will be disappointed in her, but they will not condemn her. They will be supportive and still love her, just as they were there for her when she got divorced. Mom has always had high expectations of herself, so she does not like the idea of people seeing her "failures"…and it's pretty darn hard to hide a pregnancy! She is the first to admit that she often struggles with pride, caring too much about what others think of her. And she is sad that she has disappointed her Heavenly Father. One day she will see how God will bring good out of what she thinks is bad. But for now, she is still struggling…

At almost 8 weeks, my brain and spinal cord are already well-formed. The nerve cells in my brain are expanding rapidly – over 100,000 of them are formed every minute...every single minute! Unbelievable! By the time I am term, I will have somewhere around 100 billion of them! God's creation is incredible! By the way, my head is large in proportion to my body. (It needs to accommodate my growing brain.)

Every day I am experiencing other new changes. Although my face is not fully developed yet, it is looking better, yet my eyes still look like dark holes in my head. The buds of my arms and legs are growing longer, and now my fingers and toes are beginning to separate and look more normal. Before too long, I will have tiny, tiny fingernails and toenails. How exciting!"

—⁓—

Another Decision

DECEMBER 11, 1985

Today is my second appointment with Dr. York, my obstetrician. After talking with Harland on the 23rd, he encouraged me to go ahead with the CVS test in Portland, so I had earlier called Dr. York about our decision. It involves seeing an OB/GYN doctor in Portland where he will first do an ultrasound and other tests; then if he thinks I am a good candidate, he will send me to another doctor who is the one who does the procedure at Emanuel Hospital. But the first doctor is still called the "admitting doctor" for the hospital. Confusing, isn't it? For me, too!

Right now, all I can think about is more bills and more doctors to pay. Also, pride is a part of my hesitation right now. Realizing that more doctors will notice that my marital status is "single… divorced…" makes me cringe. My appointment is scheduled for tomorrow. I plan to drive myself up to Portland, but it sure would be nice if someone would go with me. Unfortunately, Harland does not want to come along. I think he still is in shock about me being pregnant.

"I guess it is You and me, Lord. Thank You for not abandoning me. We will have a nice long talk on the way. Or, maybe not so nice! As You know, I am still having a tough time dealing with everything that is happening."

Angela: "I am now about 9½ weeks old and a little over 1½ inches long. It is incredible that even at that tiny size, all my organs are already in place. Still almost weightless (less than one ounce), I lie suspended in mom's amniotic fluid. This salty sea protects my delicate organs.

My blood now absorbs from the placenta the proteins, fats, and sugar needed for the continuous process of cell-building. The placenta is also the source of the oxygen necessary to fuel this process. By now, my teeth and taste buds are beginning to form. Aren't we all happy about both of those?

'You are amazing, Lord! How each cell knows its function is something scientists are still trying to figure out. You have created a wondrous being, one who has both body and soul!'"

—⁓—

CVS Time

DECEMBER 12, 1985

I am in my car, driving to Portland to see the doctors who will administer my CVS (Chorionic Villi Sampling) test. First, I need to find the office of Dr. Buckmaster. I am so bad with directions, and I hate Portland traffic! But at least I have 90 minutes to spend alone as I drive up there. With lots of time to think, I spend the time praying.

"Lord, am I doing the right thing by having this test? What if it shows something is abnormal with the baby? Would I really be able to abort it if it has Down's Syndrome? I already know the answer to that: I would not be able to do it because I know in my heart it is still a life You created. Yet, if I am honest with You, Lord, I must admit that if I miscarried, it would sure make life a lot easier for me. And I could hide alone with my secret - keeping it from my kids, my parents, my brothers, my nosy neighbors, my church family, my co-workers, and the multitude of others who will judge me. Lord, forgive me for these thoughts. But I want You to know that I cannot do this alone; I do not have the strength to walk through this by myself. Please tell me You will never leave me. Please, please, please! I need You! I am clinging to Your promise that You will always be with me.

And, excuse me for changing the subject, but I beg of You, will You help me find this stupid doctor's office?"

—⁓—

I found it! Hooray! But as I look around at all these pregnant women in their various stages of "blossom," my doubts return. And the paperwork. Always the paperwork. I feel like marking "married" just to keep myself from more humiliation. And the waiting is killing me. Will this doctor be kind or judgmental?

Now, I am on my way to Emanuel Hospital to see yet a different doctor, even though Dr. Buckmaster is still considered the "Admitting Doctor." At least he seemed nice - except he charged me $150 for a 3-minute visit. Luckily, I only had to make a co-pay of $30 today. I cannot imagine how much the hospital is going to charge. All I can say is thank God for insurance - and for the assurance that Harland will pay half of the remaining balance.

—⁓—

So here I am at Emanuel Hospital. As I once again *wait* after filling out *more paperwork*, I cannot help but remember that at one time, I planned on going to nursing school here at Emanuel, after attending one year at my church college. Instead, I stayed and graduated from there, and after a 7-yr marriage, I ended up divorced, with two young children to raise by myself. Two years later I went to a community college as a single parent to get my RN degree. It was so much harder to do than if I had gone to nursing school before I got married and had children.

And I cannot help but wonder how my life would have turned out if I had done as I had planned in the first place. Would I still be in this predicament? Yet, I realize I cannot change the past, and I would not trade anything for my wonderful college experiences or my two precious, precious children. (Uh, make that *three*, now)

—⁓—

This is so exciting! After getting more bloodwork - of course – and answering questions about my other two pregnancies, I met with Dr. Hagge, the one who is doing the procedure. Apparently, not many doctors have been trained to do this CVS procedure, as compared to an amniocentesis. It has only been available in the United States since 1983. A simple way to explain the procedure is this: the doctor removes a tiny bit of the chorionic tissue that will become the placenta, and they use that for genetic analysis. It is a safer alternative for women who need genetic testing early, including women 35 years and older. As I said, I am 38.

CVS can be done between the 8th-10th week gestational age of the baby. My baby is just about 10 weeks right now.

Here is the exciting part – the doctor did this procedure by using ultrasound, and I got to watch. He showed me my baby's heartbeat, which was incredible! The baby is so tiny, but I definitely could see it. So amazing! I could see it move around a bit, plus there were little arms and legs already. The doctor said I could find out the sex of the baby from this test, even though you cannot tell from today's ultrasound. I told him I would like to find out. Then he said I would hear all the results within two weeks. As sorry as I have been that I got pregnant, after today I am beginning to be a little excited!

Angela: "Mom got to actually 'see me' for the first time today on the ultrasound. Speaking of seeing, my eyes are fully formed - the cornea, iris, pupil, lens, and retina. Eyelids cover my eyes, and they won't open until much later. At almost 10 weeks, my fingers and toes are fully developed, (no more webbing) including the beginnings of the tiniest little fingernails and toenails. I can move around a little in this nice warm place. My movements are a little jerky, but I can even flex my arms and legs a bit. Pretty cool! Sometimes, I even get the hiccups...not my favorite movement!"

—m—

Reality Sets In

DECEMBER 18, 1985

After seeing the ultrasound in Portland, I cannot deny what is going on. Surprisingly, I think seeing the baby has me a little excited. Of all things, I went out today and bought 2 maternity nursing gowns. The ones from my other two pregnancies were given away long ago. I also will soon have to think about other maternity clothes. Before too long, my pants are going to get snug around the middle. Oh, gee...am I really ready for all this?

"Lord, I know You are with me, but sometimes I do feel abandoned. Part of that may be my guilt speaking to me. I know You have forgiven me, but I feel myself withdrawing from You because of my shame. I have let You down, Lord, because when people find out, I can just hear them saying, 'I thought she was a Christian. Hmmm...She is a bad example to her children, to her church, and especially to non-believers! Tsk, tsk, tsk...'

"Lord, I wonder how I can be so afraid, guilty, and excited all at the same time. Am I going crazy? Or is it the hormones?"

Angela: "I am glad Mom is beginning to be excited at this point. She has had to make some hard decisions, and still has some difficult things ahead of her, such as telling her children and her parents - my sister, brother, and grandparents. That is exciting to think about! I wonder what they will think of me...?"

—m—

She's a Girl!

DECEMBER 23, 1985

Earlier today, I had my regular appointment with Dr. York – my third visit. As usual, Harland declined to go with me. I do not think he is ready for public acknowledgement that he is going to be a father again. Guess what! His girlfriend is still pregnant! I cannot change that.

My check-up went well and it looks like everything is good. Not only was everything looking hunky-dory with me, I finally found out what I have been anxiously awaiting - the results of my CVS test.

Some good news - my baby is a little girl! And everything about her is perfect, despite my age. Oh, how exciting! Another girl…names are already beginning to flood my mind.

"What shall we call her, Lord?"

I need to call Harland and tell him. He has three boys, so he may be excited (or as excited as he can be) to know that he will now have a little girl.

Since I will be at my mom's and dad's house for Christmas, Harland and I had a date at the end of last week to celebrate. I got him a little something. He did not get me a little something. It was more of a little nothing. He still seems interested in pursuing our relationship, but sometimes I wonder…

Dr. York also shared more from the reports sent to him by the doctors in Portland. Although I agreed to have the CVS, I knew in my heart that even if this baby had Trisomy 21 (formerly known as Down's Syndrome), I would not abort. But I was much relieved to find out that everything about her was perfect.

"Thank You, Lord! One less thing to worry about."

Angela: "Mom seems very excited to find out that I am a little girl. I wonder what she will name me. I am now just over 11 weeks old. I can bend my knees, ankles, wrists, and elbows. Besides being able to move around more, I realize I can open and close both my fists and my mouth. My bones are getting harder every day, but my skin is so thin you can see right through it to my veins. My kidneys are producing urine, my liver is making red blood cells, and my pancreas is producing insulin. Everything about me is just as God designed me to be!"

—⁓—

A "Merry?" Christmas with Mom and Dad

DECEMBER 23, 1985 (LATER THAT DAY)

Now, Amy, Andrew, and I are on our way to Pendleton to spend Christmas with Mom and Dad, my two brothers and their families. It is about a 6-hour car trip, and I will have a lot of time to think while driving (in between keeping the children entertained enough so that they won't kill each other there in the back seat of our car).

It was during this "think" time that I decided that this would be the time when I would tell my family that I am pregnant. I began running scenarios through my head. None of them seemed to turn out well. Would our Christmas be ruined because of my announcement?

Understandably for me, this normally exciting and happy time of celebrating Christ's birth was clouded over with my plan to tell my family my news. But as I am learning once again, God's plan is often much different than my own.

The kids and I always stayed with Mom and Dad, so once we got there and settled in, all the family joined us that night for dinner. The time did not seem right to just blurt out: "I'm pregnant!" at the dinner table, but my heart started pounding just thinking about telling everybody.

"Alert! Deodorant fail!"

"Oh, Lord, this is going to be so hard for my family to accept. Help me do this the right way."

So, after my brothers and their families left and my children were in bed, I determined I was going to talk to Mom and Dad about my pregnancy.

Instead, they began to share with me about what had been going on with my younger brother, Rick. I was five when Rick was born, and I decided right then and there that he was *my* baby. I had never stopped thinking of him that way. Sadly, when he was in his late teens, he was diagnosed with bipolar disease. When he was on his meds, he was good to go, but when he decided to go off them, look out! And that is what had just happened! After watching some stupid TV show, he thought he had been cured, so he secretly quit taking his meds. Subsequently, he and his wife had had a terrible fight, and the police were called. No one was arrested, but the incident was not a good experience for anybody, including my parents.

Things were just now starting to settle back down, but Mom and Dad were still very stressed and upset. How could I add to their stress by telling them about me? I can't…not now…I am going to have to wait.

I know what I will do. I will talk to my older brother, Rodney, who is a pastor. I am sure he has dealt with this problem more than once during his almost 20 years of pastoring churches with his wife, Toni. He will help me find the right way to break the news to Mom and Dad.

DECEMBER 24, 1985 – CHRISTMAS EVE

My brother, Rodney, called me after lunch, and said he wanted to come over and talk to me about something. Perfect! So, after he arrived, we went to his old bedroom and sat on the bed so we could talk privately. But before I could tell him my news, he started telling me about his recent heart palpitations and episodes of chest pain. He told me he was also considering leaving the ministry because of one of the old ladies at his church in Hoquiam. Sadly, she was constantly telling him what a terrible pastor he was. She did not seem to approve of anything he did, whether it was giving his sermons, choosing the music, or running the meetings – whatever she could think of to harass him.

Oh, brother! Oh, my dear, sweet brother! This was a man who did everything at that church, including all the secretarial duties, the children's and youth programs, counseling, weddings, funerals...as well as his other duties as a pastor. Toni, his wife, was right there beside him, helping him run the church, although the church did not see fit to give her a salary. And how can one old lady be so mean...to the point of causing my brother to experience chest pains? And to give up the ministry! This is terrible!

And how can I add to his grief by telling him his favorite (and only) sister is pregnant? I can't! Not now. Nor can I tell my younger brother, Rick. You see, Rick has always idolized me a bit, and I dare not destroy his image of me, especially when he is in the recovery of his manic high. He always goes into depression afterwards, and I do not want to add my news to his burdens.

"I guess it's not the right time, Lord...You will show me how and when to break this news to my family."

DECEMBER 25, 1985 – CHRISTMAS DAY

Our family gathered together this morning to open our presents, and I could not help but think about the "present" that I had hidden within me. I was doing OK until I opened one particular gift from Mom and Dad.

First, let me tell you that I have a music box collection. Through the years, my friends and family have added to that collection on various special occasions, making each music box dear to me, not because of the box itself, but because of the precious people and occasions they represent, and the memories that come to mind when I hear them tinkle their tune.

But back to my Christmas present: When I opened my gift, I burst into tears! It was a music box of a mother holding a baby girl in her arms. Behind her was another little girl, more grown up. My first thought was that my parents knew about my future daughter. But no...the song that played was "Turn Around." "Turn around, turn around, my little one, little one..." a beautiful song about how quickly our children grow up and are soon gone. Yet as I looked at this music box, I could not help but think of my two daughters: the 11-year-old sitting across the room from me...and the baby I would one day hold in my arms.

My mom and dad, knowing that I am a sensitive soul, thought I cried because…well…because I always cry when things touch my heart. Never would they have guessed the real reason behind my tears!

Angela: "Now I am 11¹/₂ weeks old, and Mom still has not told her family about me. My development continues: at this point, I no longer rely on the yolk sac for blood cell formation: now my liver and spleen have taken over the job. Soon, my bone marrow will start producing blood cells, where the white cells will further develop in my lymph glands and thymus. Also, my genitals have started developing. This is exciting! I am becoming my own person, one amazing step…or should I say "cell"…at a time?!

Although my head still seems a little big for my body, I am now a little over 1¹/₂ inches from crown to rump. My eyes, nose, and mouth are looking more normal. There is still a lot of room in this cozy, warm place. I continue to jerk and move around; sometimes I do a somersault. I am still too little for Mom to feel me kick when I flex my tiny legs. Ooh! This is fun! But at times I still get those nasty hiccups - which are no fun at all!"

—∞—

Telling My Children

DECEMBER 27, 1985

The kids and I are headed home now, and things did not go as I had planned with my family. Wisely, I kept my mouth shut and will still need to find a time and a way to tell Mom and Dad – a time when life is less stressful for them. Will that ever happen? Who knows?

But there is no getting around it; I need to tell my children. I have prayed long and hard about this. I want to tell them in a way that they understand that premarital sex is against God's laws. They will have to hear that their Mommy is not perfect. (Yah, right...as though they really thought that about me). But it is still going to be hard to tell them. At ages 11 and 9, they are old enough to know about sin and making wrong choices. But still, it is going to be hard to admit that I sinned in such a way. On top of that, one of my fears is about what others may say to them. Parents talk...therefore, kids talk. I want them to be excited about their new sister, not ashamed of her.

"Lord, please help me reveal my secret the right way. This is so hard for me!"

I promised myself that I would talk to them as soon as we left town. Although I am dreading it, I am going to tell them right now...

"You can do this, Renée!"

"Uh...how about when my trip odometer gets to twenty-five miles? Yes, that is when I will do it."

...Twenty-two miles – twenty-three miles – twenty-four miles... my stomach has been slowly sinking while the odometer has been slowly rising...I just cannot do it yet!

43

"How about when we reach 50 miles?"

Nearing 50 miles and my heart is now pounding! I feel sick to my stomach, and this time I know I cannot blame it on morning sickness. Why is it so hard to tell my children that I am a sinner? For one, I do not want to be a bad example to them. I don't want my actions to one day be used as an excuse for their own choice of having sex before marriage. And let's be honest…I do not want them to see me as a sinner. It is pride once again raising its ugly head.

"Lord, please give me the right words – words that speak truth – words that will move their hearts to acceptance of their new sister, yet words that will not give approval of my actions." So here goes:

"Amy and Andrew, Mommy needs to talk to you about something. You know that I have been dating Harland for several months now. He and I did something that is not right in God's eyes. God tells us in the Bible that people should wait until we marry to be intimate. But we did not wait. Yes, Mommy sinned. Despite this, God is giving us a gift. We are going to have a baby. You are going to have a new sister sometime around July 15th. So, what do you think about all this? Would you like a baby sister?"

—⁓—

One thing about children is that they are not only non-judgmental, they are very forgiving. To my surprise, my kids were excited about the idea of having a new sister. As we talked about what was happening, we decided that since we knew she was a little girl, we should go ahead and give her a name.

I told them I was thinking of calling her Angela Joy. Then I told them that when I was around their age, the next-door neighbors at my parents' house had a little baby girl who they named Angela. Ever since I can remember, I have loved babies! When Angela was born, I was out of school for the summer, so I was in heaven! A baby girl, right next door! I was over there every day…or as much as my mom would let me go. Angela's mom was in fact very thankful for my help, letting me give

Angela a bath, change her diapers, and even feed her a bottle and burp her. It was the best summer!

Then I told Amy that Angela was one of the names that her dad and I had considered when she was born. I also told them that one of my best friends from college named her daughter Joy, and that I wanted their new sister to always know that her birth brought much joy.

They both agreed that Angela Joy was a perfect name for their little sister.

Angela: "Wow! Mom just found out less than a week ago that I am a girl and already I have a name! Angela Joy! I like it. And I am so thankful that when my mom hears my name, it will bring good thoughts to her mind. At the end of this week, I will be 3 months old, and it is nice to know my name. Angela Joy! I like to keep saying it...

Speaking of hearing, during this past month, my external ears started to grow. They began with a tiny fold of skin forming by the side of my head. I wonder if they will look more like Mom's or Dad's. Oh, goodness! It does not matter...they both have good ears. By the second month, my brain and spinal cord are already well-formed, although my head is still a little large in proportion to the rest of my body. (Maybe that is why I am already worrying about how my ears are going to look. Ha! Ha!)

To change the subject, I am excited about being able to wiggle my fingers and toes, which are now complete with the tiniest nails. Remarkably, my fingers are beginning to develop my own personal fingerprints! My weight by this time is only about 2 ounces. I am just over 2 inches long. And I have a name!"

—∞—

An Unexpected Revealing

JANUARY 9, 1986

I cannot believe what happened at work today. First, let me tell you a little about my job. I am a Registered Nurse, working 28 hrs/week, which translates into three 8-hr shifts one week and four the next. I work on an orthopedic floor, so we have a great variety of patients. Hospital policy at this time is that if you are pregnant, you do not take care of any patients who are positive for hepatitis B.

Well, sure enough it happened. We were all in the nurses' "report" room, getting our assignments for the day. One of the patients given to me was a patient who had had knee surgery.

"Oh, and by the way, he is (+) for hepatitis B," the charge nurse added.

I was just not ready to tell people at work about my pregnancy. One of the things I was concerned about was my Christian witness. They all know that I am a Jesus-follower, and I did not want to give Christians a bad name by my disobedience. And let me be honest, my pride was kicking in, and I did not want to face the embarrassment I knew I would feel at being pregnant but not married. Humble pie has never been my favorite…

So, hoping no one would hear but the charge nurse, I quietly spoke up. "Uh…I can't take that patient."

"Why not?"

"Well, you see…I'm pregnant…"

Suddenly, the report room became deathly quiet as people reacted in shock over my announcement. As I sat there, feeling my face begin to redden, that moment of silence seemed to last forever. Finally, one nurse bravely said, "Congratulations!" And people, including me, breathed again.

My assignment was then changed, and believe me, that shift was very uncomfortable for everyone. Nobody said a word to me about my current situation, except for one close friend.

"Oh, Lord Jesus, I am so sorry to have dishonored You with my witness to my fellow nurses. I pray that my correct handling of this unexpected pregnancy will lead to something positive. Only You can bring good from this difficult situation. Help me to say and do the right things. And please, if You see fit, will You give me an understanding friend at work, someone who will support me through this difficult time? Thank You, Jesus."

Angela: "During this past month I have made many changes. I am now almost 2¹/₂ inches long, and I weigh about 2¹/₂ ounces. My external ears are looking more complete. Hidden in my tiny jawbone are itty-bitty beginnings of my teeth. More incredible, my ovaries already are full of ova (female eggs)! My hair follicles have started developing deep in my skin, but they won't produce hair until I am almost 20 weeks.

I have begun swallowing amniotic fluid, so I am now peeing. Plus, my bowels have begun making meconium, which will eventually be my first poop. (Sorry about the peeing and pooping remarks.)"

—∿—

One Day...Kindergarten?

JANUARY 15, 1986

Last night, the kids and I went to a pizza parlor with my friend Marilyn and her two children. While we were waiting for the pizza to come, the children all went over to the inside play area, which has not only things to climb, but also a video arcade area. That gave Marilyn and me a chance to talk. She and I are both nurses, and she occasionally works on my floor. During the past few months, we have become good friends. She too is a Christian, a single-mother, and she struggles with many of the same problems that I often face. Her ex is also not in the state, so she is a mom 24/7 like I am. Of course, she is not dealing with an unexpected pregnancy...like I am...but she is a very good listener and has a very compassionate, non-judgmental heart.

Because of that, a couple of weeks ago I shared with her all that was going on with me, including the fact that I had a little girl growing inside of me. Tonight, she really helped me think differently about everything.

She said, "Renée, one day you are going to send this beautiful little girl off to kindergarten, and all of this turmoil you are going through now will be forgotten."

Wow! Now I have an image of a beautiful dark-haired, dark-eyed little girl – Angela Joy – going off to her very first day of school. It is an image I will never forget. And it makes everything seem better.

That night in bed as I prayed, I remembered one of my favorite scriptures: **"Children are a gift from the Lord." Psalm 127:3 NLT.**

Angela is a gift! I need to remember that during the next few months, as more and more people find out about my pregnancy. The Lord is going to help me get through this. He has a perfect plan. I just need to keep trusting Him.

And when things get difficult, I am going to keep that image of 5-yr old Angela at the front of my mind.

Angela: "Both Mom and Dad have dark hair and dark eyes, so it seems inevitable that I will too. And I think it is really sweet that Mom is now seeing me as a gift from the Lord. She is beginning to get the picture now! Hmmm...what is kindergarten?"

—m—

My Spending Spree

JANUARY 22, 1986

I don't know if it is because I have now told my children about Angela, or my recent conversation with my friend Marilyn, or if I am actually beginning to get excited about this unexpected pregnancy – or all of the above - but the last few days I have been buying things that have made me more enthusiastic about having another baby. One, I have realized that some of my clothes are no longer fitting well, especially my pants. So, I have bought a few maternity clothes, but right now, I am only wearing the pants with some loose tops. I am just not yet ready to reveal my pregnancy to everyone by wearing maternity tops; that will have to wait a bit. I did break down and buy some white maternity panty hose for work, as my other ones are just too tight.

Even more exciting are the things I have bought for the baby! I found the cutest little clown for her crib! You can wind up his little red nose, and he plays a sweet melody. I also bought two sheet sets for when Amy and Angela are both in twin beds. OK– I know I am jumping the gun a little, but I could not help myself, because the sheet sets match the little clown. And their room will be so cute! I can almost picture it now. I can decorate in all the primary colors. I wonder what color I should paint the walls…And who did I loan the crib to? Hmmm… I need to start thinking about these things.

Angela: "Wow! Mom is finally getting excited about me! I can't wait to meet the funny clown...and even better than that will be to meet my sister, and share a room with her. I also cannot wait to meet my brother. And Mom and Dad, of course!

I have had many changes in the past 3 weeks. First, my vocal cords have formed, and my large head is now more proportionate to my body. My eyes are fused now and will not open again until I am 7 months old. My skin has begun to thicken and fine hairs have developed over my body to help protect my skin from being in amniotic fluid constantly. My external genitals are almost fully formed now.

Not only that, I discovered that I can stick my fingers in my mouth. My sense of taste is not yet developed, so my fingers don't taste like much...but I sometimes enjoy sucking on them! My thumb seems to work the best. At this time, I am still practicing breathing in the amniotic fluid, but my lungs are only beginning to develop. Finally, one of the best things I have noticed in this last week is that I can smile! It feels pretty good!"

—⁂—

My Poor Aunt Mildred

JANUARY 25, 1986

Yesterday, I got a call from my mom. She had some terrible news to tell me. My aunt Mildred just found out she has breast cancer. She is going to have to get a mastectomy in a couple of weeks. Oh, I hate this!

My aunt Mildred lives close to me, so I know her the best of all my aunts (and I have a lot of them). She and my mom were the closest in age of all their siblings (except for the twin brothers, of course). Growing up, we often visited her and Uncle Bill. Plus, we had the coolest cousins who always took us on exciting adventures around their place in the woods. They collected interesting rocks, butterflies, and bugs, especially spiders. (The last one I could have done without.)

When I came here for college, I was six hours away from my parents, so my auntie became my "second mom" during those years. She would often have me over for a Sunday dinner of delicious, home-cooked food. She was a great cook, and her food was much, much better than the cafeteria where I ate most of my meals. I did not have a car, so she would pick me up after church. She was also good to have me over for a holiday dinner if I was unable to get a ride to go home to my parents.

Now that I am on my own, she is still good about having the kids and me over for holiday meals. She is another person who it will be hard to admit that I am having another baby, since I am not married. I think I will let my mom do the job of telling Aunt Mildred…if I ever get the nerve to tell my parents.

Anyway, it makes me sick that she has breast cancer. I know that having a radical mastectomy and doing chemo and radiation can increase the chances of winning the battle over cancer, but I still hate that she is having to face all of that.

"Lord, please be with Aunt Mildred. Give her the strength to face the battle ahead of her. Help her to know that You will be with her every step of the way. Give her peace in her heart, and please bring healing to her body. I know she believes in You and in the power of prayer. Thank You, Jesus."

—◦—

My Poor Little Snowflake

JANUARY 27, 1986

Yesterday after I got off work, I talked to my vet about my kitty, Snowflake. He is acting very sick; he hardly ate anything all weekend. Snowflake is all white (aren't we brilliant with his name)? He is the last of four babies from my cat Taffy. Taffy was young when she had her kitties, and three had been given away, but we ended up keeping Snowflake. He was special to me, because not only was he the last of the litter, I had to rescue him when he was born. He came out with his amnio sac intact, and poor little Taffy was too exhausted from having four kitties that she did not open the sac up so Snowflake could breathe. So, I had to do it (Yuk!) - although I had no idea what to do. Of course, this all happened in the middle of the night.

Just as I was getting back to sleep, I could hear a lot of mewing going on (they were born in my closet – isn't that where all kitties are born?) When I turned on the light to check on them, I found that all four kittens had their cords still attached to their "afterbirth", and their cords were all tangled up with each other. Again, I had no idea what to do about it, but this time I called my vet, despite the hour. I needed professional help, and luckily, my vet was a family friend. He told me how to cut the cords with my fingernails (double yuk) and that is when I noticed that one of Snowflake's legs was all tied up in another kitty's cord. If I had not heard the crying, Snowflake would have probably lost one of his legs. All this to say: Snowflake was very special to me, and now he was sick, and not eating.

My vet told me about a new disease that is killing a lot of cats called feline leukemia. They now have a vaccine, but Snowflake had not been vaccinated yet because he was too young. After work today, I am taking him to the vet for some bloodwork, IV fluids, and they will probably keep him overnight for observation. Another medical bill…this time not mine.

"Lord, I cannot lose my kitty…please save him."

I am having one stress after another during this pregnancy. First, my favorite aunt has cancer, then my kitty may die. If it's not one thing, it's something else!

Angela: "It may seem silly to you that Mom is worried about her kitty when she is dealing with so many other things that are so much more important. But she loves hard when she loves, whether it is her family, her friends, or her kitties. And I know she already loves me very much too.

At 16 weeks, several things are changing in my body. My lips are now formed, which will certainly help me when I learn to talk. And my smile will be even better! Now my ears have developed enough that I can hear my mom talking. Soon I will begin to recognize her voice, as well as the voices of my sister and brother. They often talk to me, too, but of course, I do not understand them.

Although my eyes are still closed as they continue to develop, sometimes I will turn away from light if it surprises me, or is very bright."

—〰—

A Tragic Day

JANUARY 28, 1986

8:30 AM

I woke up earlier than usual because I wanted to get the kids on the school bus so I could be ready to watch on TV the Space Shuttle Challenger take off this morning at 8:38 PST. The kids get to watch at school.

I am excited about today because we have been hearing about this launch on and off for months. You see, this is the first time someone other than an "official" NASA astronaut will be on board. Christa McAuliffe, a social studies teacher from New Hampshire, is getting to go with the astronauts on the flight. She has been training with them for months, so that is why this launch is getting so much publicity. They are calling this the "Teacher in Space Project." Christa is going to be talking to school children "live" about her experiences in space. The crew is going to deploy a communications satellite and study Halley's Comet while they are in orbit. It is all very exciting! Christa has been interviewed on TV so much that I almost feel like I know her personally. Her family, too...she is married and has two children, ages 6 and 9, who are all watching from the roof of the nearby Launch Control Center.

This launch was originally scheduled for January 22nd, and has been delayed a couple of times already. The weather has not been cooperating, but today is looking good! I cannot wait! Let me grab another cup of coffee before it starts. Ooh...it is almost time!

8:41 AM

Oh, my gosh! What just happened? The lift-off was at 8:39 PST (one minute later than scheduled) but less than 2 minutes later, the spacecraft literally blew up! It just disintegrated before my very eyes! They are saying that it was only 73 seconds into the flight when it exploded. I cannot believe it!

"Oh, Lord, now they are saying that everyone on board was killed!"

My stomach hurts just thinking about all their families who were watching. And poor Christa – and the other six crew members. This is the first time there has been a fatal accident in our space program. My gosh! I just cannot believe it! I know I am repeating myself, but this just does not seem real!

Oh no, the kids are going to be so upset when they get home. They have been watching the whole thing at school. I bet they will cancel the rest of the school day. I'm sure I will get a phone call about when to expect the bus today.

11:30 AM

I cannot tear myself away from the TV. They just repeat showing the explosion over and over again. But something that is really scaring me is that when I just went to the bathroom, I found some bloody spotting. I have a call into Dr. York, so I am waiting to hear back from him.

12:00 PM

The kids just got home from school. As I expected, they were very upset about the Challenger. I had to comfort them, pretending to be strong although I was so upset myself. Plus, I had another episode of spotting, and I felt a twinge or two that felt like a mild contraction. As soon as I fix the kids lunch, I am going to call Dr. York's office again. Then I'm going to have the kids play in the toy room for a while. They do not need to see any more television right now. But I do…I'll turn the TV volume way down so the kids can't hear it.

1:00 PM

Twenty minutes ago, I got admitted to Sacred Heart Hospital. The more I watched the news about the Challenger explosion, the more stressed I got. I should have turned off the TV, but I could not make myself stop watching. I don't know if this explosion is the reason this happened, but not only did I have more spotting, I still was feeling some mild contractions. They were not terribly painful or regular, but when Dr. York called me back, he told me to come to the office so he could see what was going on. I called Grandma Jessie to come over to babysit the kids, and luckily, she was home and lives just around the corner. I felt bad about leaving Amy and Andrew when they were already upset about the Challenger explosion, but I do not want to lose my baby. I tried to reassure them that everything was going to be OK, but I admit I am scared.

After examining me at his office, Dr. York decided to send me to the hospital emergency room, where he would meet me. He wanted me to get a better ultrasound because he was concerned about the bright red blood. Angela is only 16 weeks gestationally, so we both knew that this is way too early for her to be born, if that is what is happening.

After Dr. York met me at the ER, he decided to admit me for observation, even though the ultrasound showed that Angela still had a nice, strong heartbeat. She was moving around in there and did not look stressed out. I was still afraid, but one positive thing happened - I got to see her suck her little thumb.

Soon I was wheeled off to the maternity floor, where I was put into a labor room, just in case things progressed. Dr. York wants to give me a continuous IV drug, Ritodrine, to try to stop my contractions. He told me it was in a category of drugs called tocolytics - drugs that inhibit contractions in pre-term labor. Hopefully, it will help my uterus to calm down.

He reassured me that my contractions were mild and that my cervix was not dilated at all. Angela still has a nice, strong heartbeat, but Dr. York knew that if the contractions continued, it was way too soon for her to be born. So here I lie, hooked up to an external fetal monitor, listening nervously to every "swish-swish" of this precious child's heart. And to think that at one time I did not even want her.

2:00 PM

Oh, man…that drug they gave me has made my heart race like crazy; it feels like it is beating out of my chest! My hands are shaky, and I feel jittery all over! I told the nurse, and she said she would let the doctor know. She did tell me that my contractions have decreased in intensity and frequency, which is good news. She will inform Dr. York to see if we can change to an oral medication of the drug.

4:30 PM

Dr. York came in to examine me and because I am not dilated and my contractions have stopped, he is sending me home with the oral version of ritodrine. He wants me to stay on bedrest as much as possible for the next few days. I told him I was scheduled to work Friday. He said if I had no more contractions or spotting, that would be okay, if I took it easy the rest of the weekend. What a relief to get out of here!

5:30 PM

On the way home, I picked up some "take-home" hamburgers and fries for the kids and me. I am keeping the TV off! After thanking Grandma Jessie, I explained to the kids that I needed to rest as much as possible for the next few days, and they vowed to help as much as they could. Whew! What a day this has been! I am looking forward to this one being over.

Angela: "Mom is worried about what happened today. It was an ordeal, but I am OK. Being pregnant with me has not been the easiest time for her. But I am so glad that she decided to have me!"

—◦—

Telling My Parents

FEBRUARY 1, 1986

No more spotting or contractions, even after working yesterday. My plan is to rest as much as possible this weekend. So, everything seems back to normal…if I can ever call my life "normal!" Now other things have surfaced in my mind. There is no way around it; I have put this off for far too long. I am going to have to tell my parents about Angela before they get here on February 21st for Amy's birthday on the 22nd. I no longer can hide my expanding waistline, and I cannot have them ringing the doorbell and then seeing their daughter almost 5 months pregnant! Not a good way to surprise them!

My parents are very loving to all of us children, but they are also very religious. And they have a strong relationship with Jesus. So, they have some definite opinions about right and wrong - because they have read the Bible, and they know God's opinion about sin. They taught us the 10 Commandments when we were very little, and took us to Sunday School and church every week growing up. Unfortunately for me, they seemed to think that sex outside of marriage is one of the worst sins ever. I know God does not rank sin – sin is sin - but in the eyes of my parents, sex is way up there at the top of "no-no's."

Most of all, I think they will be hurt, even more than they will be disappointed in their only daughter. I want to neither disappoint nor hurt them, but I know I will do both when I tell them.

I have prayed long and hard about how to do this. A phone call seems a little bit awkward, especially since they are 6 hours away and they will not be able to read my facial expressions…or my heart …nor I, theirs.

I think the best way to do this is to write them a letter, especially so they can see my heart as expressed in words. Maybe I can make them see how lonely I have been for so many years, and how more than anything, I have wanted to feel loved by someone. I know it does not excuse my behavior, but maybe they will see why I succumbed to temptation.

Then I will ask them to call me so we can talk about it over the phone before they come. I know they are going to be so upset, no matter how they find out.

As I prayed about this, God gave me another idea. I am going to first send a letter to their pastor, who is a very compassionate man with whom they have a close relationship. I am going to share my situation with him, and ask him to be there for them – not to tell them, but to give them the encouragement they need to deal with a pregnant, unmarried daughter, whom they love very much and want the best for.

So, that is just what I do. I have written two letters, and I am sending the one to their pastor today, and I will send the one to my parents on Monday. I will know exactly when Mom and Dad receive their letter, because my phone will ring ten minutes later. I still am dreading it, though.

"Lord, will You please be with my parents and help them receive this letter with the love with which it was intended? And will You please remind them of grace? And forgiveness? And unconditional love? I know it is a lot to ask for. More than anything, please let them feel Your presence and Your peace. Remind them that You are still in control and everything will be okay. Thank You, Jesus…"

—⁓—

FEBRUARY 8, 1986 - 9:30 PM

My phone is ringing, and I just know it is my parents. I had to work today, and my babysitter told me they had called and talked to the kids while I was at work. So, I know what is coming. At least the kids are in bed so I can talk more freely. A quick prayer, then I cautiously say, "Hello…"

—⁓—

I was right. It was Mom and Dad. It went better than I thought it would, although Mom, especially, let me know that sex outside of marriage was not right. I reassured her that I had also read the Bible, and that I was sorry to have disappointed them...and God.

They really have felt hurt by my actions, and I know it will be embarrassing for them when their friends at church find out. They did not say that in words, but I know it is part of what they are dealing with.

I did not try to justify my actions – well, maybe I did a little bit – but I did bring up the fact that I could have had an abortion, and I chose not to destroy my baby. I also told them she was a little girl, and that the kids and I had named her Angela Joy. I wanted them to think about their new granddaughter, even though they did not like the circumstances of her conception.

All in all, it was not as bad as I expected...or imagined it would be.

"Thank You, Lord. I feel like a big burden has been lifted off of me. Finally, my parents know. And I told them they could be the ones to tell my brothers. (I know...I am a coward.) Good night, Jesus."

Angela: "I am excited that my grandparents know about me now. I look forward to meeting them someday. I hope they will learn to love me, like I know they love their daughter. And like I know their daughter loves me. Being loved is so lovely."

—∞—

Exciting developments!

FEBRUARY 9, 1986

Now that I have finally told my parents about Angela, I slept well and woke up this morning with a sigh of relief. Today was a work day, and it turned out to be an exciting one. Not anything having to do with work, but what happened there. You see, I have been waiting for those little "butterfly kisses" in my abdomen. It has been years since I have felt them but I knew immediately what they were. Yes - I felt life for the first time today!

Wow! There is nothing like those beginning little "kicks" that say, "Mom, I'm here!" The official name for this is "quickening." These little kicks feel like a fluttering butterfly in your tummy (uterus, of course). Before too long, I will be feeling some harder kicks that will perhaps make me wonder if my little girl will one day be a soccer player like her big sister and brother.

I am now 18 weeks along, and my last appointment with Dr. York was just last week (February 4th), and everything looked good, even though I had experienced a little spotting the week before. Luckily, I was only in the hospital for a few hours. And those horrible pills I took at home soon made me stop having those scary contractions. That whole thing was an unexpected event, but we think it was just that so much additional stress hit me all at once. My aunt…my kitty…the astronauts…

I still cannot believe that the Challenger rocket exploded! And that I ended up in the hospital! Hmm…I wonder how high that bill will be? Oh, well…not going to worry about it. Today is a day to celebrate! I felt my baby kick!

But back to my appointment on the 4th. First, I was told to not eat any breakfast before I came, then when I got there, they pricked my finger for my baseline blood sugar level. Next, I had to do that yucky glucose tolerance test, and drink all that sugary liquid, then get my blood tested after one hour, two hours, and three hours. They were testing for gestational diabetes, which can occasionally happen when you are pregnant because of changes in your metabolism during pregnancy. Luckily, my results were all within normal limits.

They also took blood from my vein for an alfa-fetoprotein test, commonly called an AFP. This is a protein normally made by the baby's liver, and high levels can be indicative of neural tube defects in the infant or chromosomal abnormalities. Dr. York is sending my blood sample up to Portland. He said it would take from 1-2 weeks to get the results. He is not worried because my CVS sample from earlier was normal. He also said there could be false positives. This is not a day for me to worry - I am just excited that I felt Angela kick for the first time today!

Angela: "Last week (17 weeks) my skin was covered with a whitish coating called vernix. This "cheesy" substance protects my thin skin. Now, At 18 weeks, I am covered in lanugo, which is hair that resembles peach-fuzz! 'Fuzzy-wuzzy was a bear...' Or should I say, '...was a peach'! I guess I am not very funny, am I? Anyway, this lanugo is keeping me nice and warm and is protecting my skin too. I am now beginning to put on a little fat. A fat peach! Ha! Ha!

My muscles are beginning to develop, and I am proud that I kicked hard enough that Mom could feel me for the first time. I sometimes have a sleep-wake cycle, and my best time to kick is right when Mom is trying to fall asleep. Maybe it is my way of saying, 'Good-night!'"

A Valentine's Surprise

FEBRUARY 13, 1986

Since I am scheduled to work on Valentine's Day, I surprisingly have a lunch date today with Harland to celebrate...I think. He and I have hardly been talking anymore. It is usually me who initiates the phone calls, always telling him about my doctor's visits...and of course about the day I was hospitalized for those few hours. I also called him the day I felt Angela move for the first time, because I was really excited about it. But other than that, we have not had an actual "date" in several weeks. I wonder what this is about. He wants me to meet him at the restaurant.

I am almost 4½ months along now, and I am most definitely "showing," if one were being observant. But I decide to dress for my date in something that hides my increasing girth...yet not an obvious maternity top. I don't think Harland has told his boys yet about our future daughter, and I do not want to make things difficult for him through wagging tongues before he has done so. Harland has a high profile here in town, so I am trying to be considerate of that.

Although things are strained with Harland, I dress up and try to look good for our date. I still have hopes for our relationship, but I have never pressured him to marry me, and I will not start now.

—m—

That was a surprise - and not a pleasant one at that! "Happy Valentine's Day! ...NOT!" Harland told me that he wants to be a part of our daughter's life, but that he will probably be married by the time Angela is born. What?! He says he has already been dating someone else, and they are planning on being married before July 15th. He said that his fiancée is the only one he has talked to about my pregnancy as of this time, and she has accepted the fact that he will have another child…with me.

Needless to say, I no longer had an appetite in spite of the fact it was my favorite restaurant. Talk about a low blow…

"Wow! Thank you for breaking up with me on almost Valentine's Day! So very kind of you." (I only wish I had had the nerve to say that out loud.) In truth, I hardly said a word in response - I was stunned speechless!

Angela: "I know Mom sounds sarcastic, but that is only her way of dealing with this news. Sadly, I felt her pain as she made her way out to her car. I heard the sobbing as she drove home, and again that night after my future siblings were in bed. I know she is hurting very much as she is trying to deal with this blow. Once again, she feels rejected and alone. Her prayers that night reflected her deep sorrow and desperation, as she realized that once more, she will be raising another child as a single parent. She feels so inadequate, and cries out to her Heavenly Father for His grace and mercy. Eventually her grieving turns into a restless sleep."

FEBRUARY 14, 1986

It was a rough night, but as I awoke this morning, I found a new strength and determination that I knew came from Jesus. He has always proven Himself to me in the past, faithfully providing for my other two children and me in ways that have often seemed miraculous. He will not let me down now. Whatever I must face, I know that He will give me the strength to go on, despite this painful rejection and disappointment I am feeling.

Sometimes I wonder what all this extra stress is doing to my body… let alone, my mental health… It is a good thing I can pray about things to help keep a calm spirit. Yet there are times when I still feel a lot of stress. I hope it is not affecting Angela in any way.

Now I must get ready for work…

—⁂—

Telling the "Praise Messengers"

FEBRUARY 17, 1986

It seems like I have had one stress after another. Speaking of stress, later tonight I have singing practice at church for our Praise Messenger ensemble. It is a singing group at church which I have been a part of for several years. Tonight is the night I have decided to tell them about my pregnancy, and I am dreading it. I just don't know how they will respond. Telling them feels like the last big hurdle I must jump. I was afraid the hurdle of telling my parents was the one hurdle that would knock all of us down. And yet it did not. God is faithful to us, even when we are not faithful to Him.

But back to the Praise Messengers - everyone in the group is younger than I am - young men and women just beginning to start their families. Yet I have always felt welcomed and loved and accepted by them. They have even kind of "adopted" my children and seem to love them too. I am also the only single parent in the group, but they have always been gracious towards me. I love every one of them, yet I am very fearful - and let me admit it - embarrassed - at having to tell them I am pregnant.

"Lord, You know that singing has always been a big part of my life, and that singing in this group has been such a blessing to me. And I realize that when my pregnancy begins to show, I will have to step down from this ensemble so that I do not offend anyone in our church. It will be very hard for me to give it up, for it has been one of the most encouraging things that I do. And let's face it – the group tonight may tell me they want me to quit right now. Lord, if possible, I ask for their mercy and grace to be extended towards me. And help me walk through this difficult night, as I once more make myself vulnerable to those whose reaction I fear."

—∞—

"Wow, Lord! Thank You! Things could not have gone any better than they did tonight. As hard as it was to tell everyone, and as much as I dreaded it, it all went very well. They were surprised, but not judgmental. I did not feel condemnation; once again, I felt grace. And as one young mom reminded me, **"For (we) all have sinned and fall short of the glory of God." Romans 3:23**

That is why You sent Your perfect Son to die on the cross to save us. His blood has covered our sins. Yet I know that my sin will soon become very public, and that is hard on my pride, as You know. And I know You hate pride, so I suppose this humbling experience will be for my own good, as hard as it may be (as others from church find out). Part of the refining process, I guess, to make me more like Your Son, Jesus.

Thanks for Your forgiveness, Lord, and thank You that Your grace was in the hearts of the Praise Messengers tonight. Not only did they say they would be there for me, several of the girls even offered to loan me some of their maternity clothes.

Tonight, as I drift off to sleep, I feel like another big burden has been lifted from my shoulders. Thank You, Lord! Good night!"

Angela: "At just over 19 weeks, my fingerprints are now complete. My brain now has designated places for my senses - taste, smell, hearing, touch, and vision. Soon, all these senses will be fully developed. Also, I feel like I am getting stronger every day. Mom seems to be at peace now. Maybe we will both get some good sleep tonight. "Hiccup!" Oh, no! Not again! "Hiccup!" Ooh...I don't like this one bit! "Hiccup!"

—∞—

Bedrest Again?

FEBRUARY 18, 1986

As I woke up this morning and began to reflect on last night, I realized that another big hurdle had been jumped. After telling the Praise Messengers and my parents about Angela, I now have a circle of friends and family who will support me throughout my pregnancy and after Angela is born. Of course, the Lord has always been my greatest supporter and always will be! Anyway, it feels like such a huge relief... even though Harland is no longer a part of my support system. At least he is willing to be involved with Angela after she is born, acknowledging his "fatherhood" to her.

So, I woke up feeling at peace. That is why I do not understand what happened next. As soon as I got up and went to the bathroom, I saw some bloody spotting...not a lot, but enough to scare me. I immediately called Dr. York's office and told them what had happened. They had me come in to get checked out, which I did as soon as the kids got on the school bus.

At this point, I was not having contractions nor any dilation of my cervix, but Dr. York told me that I needed to go on bedrest again, except for going potty (sorry, that's what mothers say) for the next few days to see if I can stop the spotting. He said if the spotting is brown, it is better than if it is bloody. He wants me to carefully monitor what I see every time I go to the bathroom. If I suddenly have a lot of blood, I need to immediately go to the hospital, and call him. He will meet me there.

As soon as I got home, I sat down on my kitchen floor and decided to make a few phone calls. (We only had one phone in the house, and it was attached to the kitchen wall...it had one of those extra-long cords, so I could pace when I needed to…like right now!). I realized I was going to need some help if I was suddenly going to be confined to my bed for a while.

Amy was about to turn 12 on Saturday, and Andrew was 9. The kids helped with dishes and had other chores, but they had never cooked a dinner before. I could not expect them to suddenly start making dinner every night. They can make cookies, of course, but we cannot exist just on dessert. Or could we…?

When I told my friend Connie about what was going on, she volunteered to bring us dinner tonight. (She lives just down the street from me and is one of the few neighbors who knows about my pregnancy). She also said if I would make a list, she would go to the grocery store for me. She said she would be willing to do that for as long as I needed her. What a blessing she is!

Before I could call anyone else, I got a phone call from a nursing friend from when I worked nights, Mignon. She wanted to go to lunch with me. When I told her I was on bedrest, she said she would love to bring lunch here on Thursday, and she would also like to bring dinner. That was an unexpected surprise!

"Thank You, Jesus! Your Word says You 'go before us,' and You certainly have proven that to me so many times during this pregnancy. Please bless Connie and Mignon for their kindness to me."

After I got off the phone with Mignon, I realized that my parents are coming this Friday to help celebrate Amy's birthday, so I knew this week was good for dinner.

So here I am…I have been on bedrest all day in my bedroom, a little bit bored with just a radio to keep me company. The good news is that my spotting is no longer bloody, but is brown. I guess I just need to rest more during this pregnancy, but it is a hard job when you are a single mom, working 3-4 shifts a week as a nurse. Speaking of that, I realize I am scheduled to work this weekend, so let's hope things improve before then. I guess all the cleaning I was planning to do before Mom and Dad come will just not get done. Oh, well… I am sure they have seen dust before…

Also, this will be the first time I will see them since I told them I am pregnant. I wonder how all that will go. I guess I just need to trust the Lord that my parents will give me grace and accept me the way I am... with a very definite protruding belly. The only reason I can still hide my pregnancy at church is that it is still winter, and I have a big coat that hides a lot. I don't take it off. Eventually, everyone will know, and that is something I am not looking forward to. (I know, Dad - "Never end a sentence with a preposition.") Dad was an elementary principal for years... so our grammar had to be correct.

Angela: "Mom is blessed with many good friends, isn't she? I believe she knows that without the Lord, her family, and her friends she would have a very difficult time being pregnant and unmarried. She made a difficult choice from the beginning...and I am so happy she did!"

—m—

The Dreaded Doorbell

FEBRUARY 21, 1986

The past two days have been good. The spotting has stopped, and I have at least done some laundry to catch up before Mom and Dad get here. They are on their way, and should be here in a couple of hours. Even though we have talked on the phone again since I first told them about Angela, I still am dreading the doorbell a little bit. When they see my belly, I think the reality of my pregnancy will hit them square in the face. Or in their gut…

We are celebrating Amy's birthday tonight, since I am scheduled to work all weekend at the hospital. Dr. York said it was OK to work as long as I took it easy and was no longer spotting. We'll see… I was able to make a cake for Amy today…chocolate, of course! She helped me frost it after school. Tonight will be a quiet celebration.

I feel the Lord is saying to me: "Just remember, Renée, take one step at a time. That is all you need to do."

For now, I am going to start praying before I hear the "dreaded doorbell."

—◊◊—

"Ding-dong…"

—◊◊—

9:30 PM

I am now in bed because I need to get up at 5:30 in the morning to go to work. Things went better than I expected with my parents tonight. It was very awkward when I first opened the door. It was like no one knew exactly what to do, so there was a big pause instead of the hugs that normally would have immediately occurred. But soon the hugs and kisses were given all around. Of course, Amy and Andrew were thrilled to see their grandparents, who we had not seen since Christmas. It was hard "not noticing" my parents "not noticing" my expanding belly.

I had fixed them an easy dinner, and while we ate, we had a nice "normal" dinner conversation because of the children. Which means…we did not discuss my pregnancy. I had already told them that the kids knew all about Angela.

After dinner we played a game with the kids and had a fun time. We sang "Happy Birthday" to Amy and enjoyed cake and ice cream. (How can you not enjoy chocolate?) Then Amy opened her presents. Once the kids headed off to bed and the prayers were said, I shared with Mom and Dad about the fact that Harland and I were no longer dating and that his plan is to be married (to someone else) by the time of Angela's expected birthdate of July 15th.

I also told them about the incident on the 26th when I was in the hospital for a few hours because of some bloody spotting and mild contractions. I said I was doing OK now, but I was supposed to take it easy as much as possible. I explained that I am still trying to keep up my work schedule because I want to save my sick time for when Angela is born. A little part of me wondered if they hoped I might lose Angela so they would never have to tell anyone about my pregnancy. Knowing them, though, I believe they will accept this grandchild and love her like they love all their grandchildren…which is a whole lot!

Of course, before we ended our conversation, Mom could not help herself – she reminded me that sex outside of marriage is wrong in God's eyes. I reassured her that I was well aware of that fact. And in the end, both of my parents reassured me that they loved me and would be there for me.

Time for sleep…

Angela: "Mom really has needed to see her mom and dad, my grand-parents. I know they will be supportive of her because they love her so much. They may not agree with her decision to sleep with my dad, but they will still be there for her, now and after I am born."

—⁂—

Bedrest...not AGAIN!

SUNDAY, FEBRUARY 23, 1986

I worked yesterday (Saturday) without any problems, then towards the end of my shift today (Sunday), I went to the bathroom and had bloody spotting again. When I told my charge nurse, she sent me home immediately. Mom and Dad were already gone when I got home at 2:15 PM. They had taken the kids to church in the morning, fed them lunch, then headed back home. They would not get there for several hours so I could not reach them yet.

The kids had left me a note saying they were playing at Connie's house. I know they were not expecting me home for another hour, so I decided I should first call Dr. York's service, which I did. Luckily, Dr. York was "on call" today, so I was thrilled it was someone who knew what had been going on. My spotting was brown again, which was a good sign. But Dr. York told me he wanted me to go on complete bedrest this time. He recommended that I take off work until we could get Angela to a more viable age. That would still be several weeks from now.

When I got off the phone, my first reaction was panic! How can I take off work? I will be using up all my sick time that I hoped to save for Angela's birth. And how do I stay on bedrest and still take care of the kids? When I finally calmed down, I realized I needed to make some plans. I needed to figure out how I could work everything out to stay in bed and do everything else I needed to do. At first, I did not know how to make it all happen. It seemed impossible. Then instead of worrying, I decided to pray.

"Lord Jesus, what is Your solution? I know You have already worked everything out. I just need to see with Your eyes. Please help me open my mind and my heart to Your will. You make the impossible possible. This I believe with all my heart. Please give me Your peace and Your vision. Amen."

After my prayer, I had a calm spirit and some ideas started coming to me. One, I needed to ask my mom if she could come back for a while and help me out with the kids, meals, etc. Mom and Dad only have one car, so Dad would have to bring her back and leave her here. It seems ironic that the first person who came to mind to help me was the one person who I was the most afraid to inform about my pregnancy. I still had to wait a couple of hours before they would get home.

Next, I thought about my friends. I am blessed with many good friends who have helped me walk through many difficult things (and whom I have tried to help when they needed me). It was time to call on them, even though I hated to do it. The girls in the Praise Messengers came to mind. I was already wearing some of the maternity clothes they had loaned me, so I called one of the wives in the group, Lynn. She immediately said that she would talk to the other wives and try to set up a meal plan for us for our dinners. She knew everyone would be willing to help if asked. She volunteered to bring dinner tomorrow night. She said that if they each brought a dinner to last us two or more nights, she was sure they would be able to be responsible for Mondays, Wednesdays, and Fridays. She said she would let me know after she talked to the other wives.

I also called Connie to let her know I was on bedrest once again. I asked her to pray for Angela and me. I also called Meredith and asked her to pray. She said she would have been more than glad to help us out, but she and her husband are still back East for a few more months. She said she had sent me a little package for Angela on Saturday. I should get it this week. That was a positive that gave me a little boost. Also, Amy and Andrew said they would help as much as they could.

I also called my charge nurse at work, and told her I was going to be on bedrest for several weeks, so she needed to take me off the schedule for now. I decided to go ahead and use my sick leave time until it runs out. I am all right until March 10th, and hopefully, I will not need to stay on bedrest that long.

7:00 PM

Mom and Dad called to let me know they got home OK, so I told them what was happening. I said that the next couple of weeks were good because of friends helping (Lynn had called me back and said they had the next two weeks covered). So, I asked if they could come back the following week. Mom said that they were already planning on coming back Wednesday night, March 4th, because Aunt Mildred was going to be discharged from the hospital after her mastectomy and Mom was planning on helping her when she got home from the hospital. She said Dad would have to go back that Sunday but she would stay if I still needed her to help. She also said they would be praying, and she would let my brothers know, so they could be praying for us too.

With the next 3 weeks taken care of, I fell into a much-needed deep sleep…but not before thanking the good Lord for giving me such sweet friends and family.

Angela: "At 20 weeks, the parts of my brain that are responsible for my 5 senses are fully developed now. I am beginning to recognize my mom's voice. My uterus will also be fully formed this week. The eggs in my ovaries are still very primitive, but now I now have close to 7 million of them. As I grow, the number will decrease dramatically. I am just over 9 inches long (measuring from my head to my heel), and getting a little fatter each day."

—⁂—

Blessings Abound!

FRIDAY, FEBRUARY 28, 1986

The Praise Messengers have been great about visiting me while I am on bedrest at home. As they arranged, they have brought dinners to us 3 times this week, and they are scheduled again next week. Because of their kindness, I decided to be brave enough to call my pastor and tell her what is going on. I could possibly be on bedrest for several weeks, and I know she (our pastor is a woman) would be wondering where we were, since we are usually there every other Sunday. (Actually, the kids are there every week. Because I must work every other weekend, a friend picks the kids up on the Sundays I work.)

Anyway, I called my pastor three days ago. We talked for a long time, and she was very supportive of me and my situation. Today I received this beautiful hand-written letter from her:

February 25, 1986

Dear Renée,

There are some things I want you to know, now that we've talked.

One — you are and will be ever present in my mind and heart, in my prayers and in the concerns that shape my day.

Two — I have a deep respect for how you are genuinely struggling with your situation. As you talked today, I sensed your commitment to sense and respond to God's redemptive presence in your life.

And, three — God can and does and will take the most difficult of our personal trials and failures and shape them into opportunities for growth, service, and beauty. You must always hope and trust that God's compassion embraces you.

Let me know how I can be of support as you continue to survive and triumph in this time.

Love, Susan

That was very reassuring to me. I need all the support I can get. I got another nice surprise today. My brother Rod sent me a new phone so I could have one in the bedroom. It was one of those trimline phones, baby blue, that I can keep on my bedside table. Fancy… That way I will not have to get out of bed to answer the phone or make a call. A neighbor helped me get it installed.

By this time, I had also told a few more church friends about my pregnancy, Carline, Loretta, and Jackie. They were all aware that Harland and I had been dating since last July. First, I told them we were no longer an item, as he was planning on marrying someone else in a few months. They were surprised about my being pregnant, yet they were very gracious about everything, and it made me realize that my fears about condemnation are instead being replaced with love!

Isn't that the way it is with God? He fills our fears with love… When we confess our sins, He loves us. When we don't confess, He still loves us. (By the way, God already knows it all, so you might as well confess). Love is the reason He sent His Son, Jesus, to die on the cross to pay for our sins. It is all about love.

Angela: "God blesses us through His people, for people who love God love people. God is love, so all of us must keep our eyes open for ways to bless others. Jesus told His followers: 'By this everyone will know that you are my disciples, if you love one another.' John 13:35"

—∞—

To the Hospital – Again?

SATURDAY, MARCH 1, 1986

Just when I think everything is settling down, something else happens. Why is this pregnancy always so difficult? I just do not understand! It seems like every time I feel I can rest in peace, something goes wrong again.

I slept well last night and woke up with a new determination to be the best patient I could be, and to only get up when I needed to go to the bathroom. Which is where everything went wrong.

I found bloody spotting again. Worse than that, I felt sure I was having some contractions. Once again, I called Dr. York, who wanted me to meet him at the hospital for another ultrasound of the baby. He also wanted some labs and to do a stress test on the baby.

After asking a neighbor to watch the kids, I drove myself to the hospital and was admitted at 10:40 AM, then wheeled up to a delivery room (just in case). They have already drawn blood and used a catheter to do a urine culture. They want to make sure that these early contractions are not being caused by any infection.

I have already had another ultrasound, which I am happy to say showed that Angela was moving around and her heart rate was very good. She looked like she is growing like she should. Upon exam, Dr. York verified that my cervix was not dilated – praise God! But he agreed I was having some mild contractions.

Now I have two belts with sensors around my expanding belly – one to measure Angela's heartrate, the other to measure the strength of my contractions. This is called a stress test, and they told me it would take about 20 minutes to record. They look to see how much Angela's heart decreases during a contraction and how quickly it recovers. This measures any stress Angela is having. It is a good thing it is not measuring my stress, because it might blow out the machine!

—∭—

Later that day...

My labs looked ok, the stress test was negative, the ultrasound was normal. After several hours, I was discharged and told to remain on bedrest. Dr. York wants me to go back on the Ritodrine orally to see if it will stop my contractions. For now, he wants me to start keeping a record of my contractions – how often I feel them, (right now they are irregular in occurrence), how long each one lasts, and whether they become regular and increase in intensity. Also, I am to keep checking on how much spotting I have and to record the color. He warned me that this could lead to an early birth that Angela would not survive.

Something was causing my uterus to be irritable, but as of now, Dr. York could not find a reason why this was happening. He said we would just wait and see what my body would do. I pray it will behave itself. Please!

Because this is my third child, I obviously know what true labor feels like. Right now, all I can do is stay in bed and pray. Stay and pray... Many times, this is exactly what God wants us to do. It is all about trust. Trusting that God's will is always for His purposes, and for our best. That is easier said than done.

I called Mom and Dad and told them about being in the hospital today. Mom said that they are still planning on coming down here next Wednesday, the 5th, to help my Aunt Mildred. She and Dad will be staying with my aunt until Sunday, then Dad will need to go home. After Sunday, Mom will stay for at least a week with me if I am still on bedrest. She said she would love to help me out with the kids, our meals, and anything else she could do for us. Dad will need to come back to get her since they only have the one car.

I feel guilty taking Mom away from Aunt Mildred. Normally, I would be trying to bring a meal or two to my aunt at such a difficult time for her. I hate that I am on bedrest and cannot help, and instead need to be the one being helped.

It has always been much easier for me to be the "giver," rather than the "receiver." I think it may be related to when I got divorced and my pride kicked in, and I wanted to prove I could learn to do everything without help from anyone…except from the Lord. Of course, it was during that time that I had to instead learn to accept help from my friends and family. It is also the time when my faith in the Lord grew so much! He proved Himself over and over by providing for me in many unexpected ways.

Life has shown me that sometimes it is our turn to give, and sometimes it is we who need the help from someone else. A friend told me that giving always blesses both the receiver and the giver, which is true. So, when we do not allow someone to help us, we are taking away a blessing from them. Something to ponder…

Angela: "At 21 weeks, I now am covered with "lanugo"- a fine, downy layer of hair that keeps me at just the right temperature. I am also beginning to get some dark hair on my head, and my eyebrows and eyelashes are also coming in. Mom sings a lot to me and I love her voice. It comforts me.

Mom may be on bedrest but I am moving around more and more. I punch or kick her sometimes when she is trying to get to sleep…not on purpose, of course. Although Mom is stressed out, the amniotic fluid still protects me from what is happening right now to her uterus. My bone marrow is now producing red blood cells to prepare me for breathing oxygen one day. Mom knows that right now my lungs are not yet developed enough, so she is naturally worried about her contractions. She prays a lot, which brings her some peace."

—

The Dreadful Sermon

MONDAY, MARCH 9, 1986

It has now been another week of bedrest and I am tired of this. Mom is here now which is a comfort to me. Last week, not only did we get some meals provided, the girls from Praise Messengers would stay for a while and visit with me during the day. Also, one of my friends from church who is in nursing school came by and gave me a bed shampoo. She brought some equipment that made it easy. It felt like heaven to get my head really scrubbed. Those dry shampoos never seem to get your hair very clean. I am one of those people who cannot stand to have oily hair. Bed baths are bad enough, but greasy hair – too much! Yet, I realize I should not complain, especially since friends and family have really stepped in to help me.

Mom comes into my bedroom to talk with me often, but there is no good place for her to sit, so she cannot stay in my room all day long. So, when the kids are in school and I am alone, I read or I listen to an especially good Christian radio station I found. It makes me feel like I have company, and the music really lifts me up. But last week, I heard the most dreadful and discouraging sermon.

One of the pastors from a local church was preaching on 2 Samuel, chapters 11-12. It is the story of David and Bathsheba, when King David lusted after another man's wife (Bathsheba), slept with her, got her pregnant, then had her husband killed in battle to hopefully hide his sin. David then married Bathsheba, and they had the baby. David thought no one would ever find out about his sins, but he was wrong. God knew.

So, God sent Nathan to confront David, David finally acknowledged his sin, and he repented before the Lord. But there were consequences for

David's actions… (this is the part I hated) …the baby got sick and died a week later. While the baby was sick, David fasted and prayed for 7 days, asking God to save the baby. On the 7th day, David was informed that the baby died, so he "**got up from the ground. After he had washed, put on lotions and changed his clothes, he went into the house of the Lord and worshipped.**" 2 Samuel 12:20a

Then he ate. His servants asked him how could he do this? David explained, "**While the child was still alive, I fasted and wept. I thought 'Who knows? The LORD may be gracious to me and let the child live.' But now that he is dead, why should I fast? Can I bring him back again? I will go to him, but he will not return to me.**" Vs. 22-23

Was this going to happen to me? Was God going to take my child? It was a very disturbing thought. Was God warning me…or preparing me? Either way, I did not like it!

Look, I know I am a child of God, and He loves me in spite of me! I also know I sinned against the Lord when I slept with Harland. And if I am honest, I knew it was wrong and did it anyway. Would I have to lose my child, too? In my opinion, I had already walked through many tough consequences - having to tell Harland, my children, my friends, my parents, my co-workers. Not only that, my boyfriend was getting married to someone else! Is that not enough?

I did not know the answer to that question. I do know that many children are born every day from sexual relationships outside of marriage. I also know that many people lose babies, and it has nothing to do with sin. So, it is obvious that God does not take every child because of sin, but the fact that He took David and Bathsheba's baby was something I did not want to hear. Anyway, I was very disturbed by that sermon, and could not get it out of my mind…especially as I was lying in bed, timing my early contractions.

I have a little notebook where I am recording every contraction. It is discouraging because although the contractions are not very strong or very regular, they keep happening. Sometimes it is only 4-5 minutes between them; other times I can go for an hour or more without any. Amy will sometime lie in bed with me after school and help me time them. One time I found a note she left me: "Once after a contraction I felt your stomach and it felt real hard where the baby was but now it is soft." I hate that she knows she might lose her baby sister. We still keep praying that all will be well.

WEDNESDAY, MARCH 13, 1986

I saw Dr. York yesterday. Angela's heartbeat was still very good, but there was bad news. My cervix is beginning to thin, and is on the cusp of starting to dilate. Dr. York tried to prepare me for an eminent early birth…and death.

It's almost midnight and I am in bed, crying, unable to sleep. I feel so alone right now. Mom and the kids are asleep, so the house is quiet…too quiet. Earlier today, as much as I hated to do it, I made arrangements for a babysitter if I go into full labor at night. Mom has already told me she wants to be there with me for Angela's birth. My friend Loretta lives fairly close to me, and she said she will come, no matter what time of night it is. So here I lie, with only my notepad to keep me company. I keep praying, but right now I am without hope. I truly do want this baby girl, but I feel very helpless as to what is going to happen.

Angela: "I am still changing every day and continue to experience new things. My grasp is stronger now, and I can now touch my ears and my umbilical cord. I can hear Mom's heartbeat, her breathing, and her stomach rumblings. Of course, I do not yet realize what I am hearing. Although I am almost 23 weeks, my lungs are not developed enough to sustain my life if I am born now. I do not know what is going to happen to me, but I do know I am in God's hands. He has made me and has a purpose for my life, just as He does for every life He creates."

—∞—

Angela is Born!

SATURDAY, MARCH 15, 1986 - 2:30 AM

Sometime during the night, my contractions increased in frequency, duration, and strength. I woke up my mom and told her I thought the baby was coming. We had a plan in place, and my friend Loretta was going to babysit the kids in case I had to go to the hospital. But then Mom told me she did not feel comfortable driving my car, so when I called Loretta, she said she'd take me to the hospital if we could get Jackie to come and stay with the kids. Time seemed to slow down as we waited for my friends to arrive. My contractions remained strong and steady. While we were waiting, I called Dr. York, who said he would meet us at the hospital.

Then I prayed so very, very hard, "This is too early, Lord! She is too small! Can't You stop this? Please! Please! I can't lose her now! Not after everything!"

Before I left for the hospital, I called Harland and told him I was in heavy labor and was headed to the hospital. It looked like our baby girl was going to be born tonight. I asked him if he wanted to come to the hospital to see her. He declined, which honestly, did not surprise me. I am sure he was relieved that he would not ever have to acknowledge this child to anyone.

As soon as we arrived at the emergency room, Mom ran in and told the nurses I was having my baby. They met me with a wheelchair, with greetings of: "Your baby is coming! Congratulations! How exciting!"

Then I told them I was only 23 weeks along, and my baby was probably not going to live. That broke the mood. I was quickly admitted and wheeled up to the maternity ward. Loretta went back to my house to babysit Amy and Andrew so Jackie could go on home.

After getting a quick history from me, the labor and delivery nurses immediately moved me to a labor room. Boom, boom, boom…things started happening too fast for me, especially in my anxious mental state.

The next thing I knew, the nurse had whisked my clothes off, put me in a gown, started an IV, checked my cervix, and hooked me up to an external fetal monitor. Because I was only 23 weeks along, the nurse was not able to use an internal monitor on me. Once she showed me how to read the monitor printout, I could see Angela's heartbeat, strong and steady. And I would not take my eyes off of that indicator of life. Even the contractions became secondary to watching the beat, beat, beat of my baby's heart. My mom stayed at my bedside, wringing her hands and praying. Isn't that what we so often do? We pray, but we also wring our hands in fear…

Soon, Dr. York arrived. After greeting me, he checked my cervix. He said I was already dilated to 8 cm, and the contractions were not going to stop. He told me that there was absolutely nothing he could do about it at this point. He was also preparing me for the inevitable outcome this early in pregnancy. He told me Angela's lungs would not have been developed enough to sustain her life. He said she would probably only live for a few minutes. I still prayed for God to do something!

3:30AM

My labor continues strong and steady, and I plead with Dr. York to stop it somehow!

"Please! Please! Isn't there something you can give me to stop this from happening? She is just too little! I don't want her to die!"

"Please, God! Save this child now, before it is too late!"

3:42 AM

Angela Joy is born, in spite of my protestations to Dr. York and the Lord! When I saw her, I was totally stunned! The first thing I said was, "Oh, my God! She is so very tiny!" I had never ever imagined someone so small!

As Dr. York lifted her up and asked me if I wanted to hold her for a minute, I almost could not look at her. That sounds horrible, I know, but I was in shock at seeing such a tiny person. At that point, Angela was still attached to my placenta. In spite of my apprehension, I said "yes," and he placed her on my chest. I was so afraid she was going to die right then and there, and I knew my heart just could not deal with that. I do remember foolishly asking Dr. York if he couldn't just put her back in.

I then gave her back much too quickly, and Dr. York cut her cord and gave her to the nurses, who quickly rushed her to the NICU, the Neonatal Intensive Care Unit. He warned me not to have hope; there was nothing they could do to keep her alive for very long. But they would clean her up, weigh her, and at least have a NICU doctor evaluate her.

4:00 AM

The most horrible and ironic thing happened after Angela was born - Dr. York kept waiting for my placenta to release itself and it wouldn't! It was like my body was reading my heart, and it just did not want this pregnancy to be over. Finally, he had to reach in and manually pull it out. Oh, my gosh! That hurt more than any labor pain I suffered with any of my babies! It was like a final injustice and insult from my body.

Then he asked if I wanted a shot to help dry up my milk that my body would produce naturally, following the birth of a child. Apparently, my body would not know she died. Of course, I said "yes." I did not want to have to face having milk with no baby to feed. He did warn me it did not always work.

5:30 AM

The nurse just gave me the shot to dry up my milk. Then Dr. York came in and told me that the NICU doctor had examined Angela - and he agreed she was too premature to live. A nurse would be assigned to her until she passed away. Then he told me he was going to discharge me this morning after I ate breakfast. He said his office would call me to schedule a follow-up appointment with him. Before he left, he expressed his sympathy to me and gave me a hug.

7:00 AM

Mom has been sitting with me since I got to my room. We both are shedding tears as we face the reality of the loss of a child and a grandchild. We are silent, because what can you say? I am in a fog; nothing feels real right now. I keep asking my nurse to call the NICU to see if Angela has died. As of now, she is still alive.

Oh, here comes my breakfast. My stomach hurts; my heart hurts; my uterus hurts. Who can eat? But mom needs to eat because of her diabetes. So I gave her my meal.

7:30 AM

The nurse came in and told me I had a visitor. For a minute, I thought maybe Harland had come after all. But no – it was someone from a funeral home in town. My precious baby Angela had not even died yet, but someone had already called him, knowing she would die soon. I hated that! It seemed cruel!

I will say that he was very kind and loving as he explained to me that, in this hospital, when a baby was born older than 20 weeks (Angela was 23 weeks), it was up to the mother to take care of making arrangements for the body. Oh, gee! I had not even thought about what would happen to her after she died. He explained there were two options - she could be cremated, or I could get a casket and bury her. He told me that there was a special place at Rest Haven Memorial Park for babies who had died. I did not know what to do; I was not even thinking clearly at this point. I mean, she was still alive! What if there was a miracle?!

I finally said she could be cremated, although I really did not like that option. He left some information with phone numbers to reach him; he also left papers I was to sign and leave with the nurses before I went home. Honestly, I was still in shock, and not ready to deal with any of this.

After he left, the nurse brought in some discharge papers with some instructions for my home care. She also gave me a birth certificate with Angela's weight, length, etc. It even had her tiny, little footprints on it. She only weighed 14 ounces – not even a pound - and was 10 inches long.

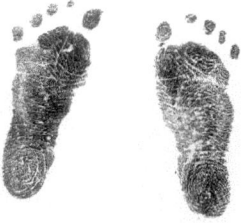

There were also some pamphlets and a little booklet called, "When Hello means Good-bye." I was not ready to deal with that yet. She told me that after the shift change, I could go up to the NICU and hold Angela and tell her goodbye before going home. Mom and I did not have a car here, so I had to call Loretta to see when she could come get us. She said she could come in about an hour. She needed to find someone to stay with Amy and Andrew, because she had an appointment at 10 AM. I knew my kids would be upset at losing their sister, so I gave her Grandma Jessie's number because I knew she would come over and stay with the kids until Mom and I got there.

Gosh! I have not even thought about that. I have to tell my kids that their little sister isn't going to live.

"Lord, how can I do that? I need Your help so I can find the right words to say to them. Please prepare their hearts to accept this. I know they have been so looking forward to welcoming their little sister home. Please help me, Lord Jesus!"

8:15 AM

My nurse took Mom and me to the NICU where Angela was still hanging on. Angela's nurse came and talked with us, then she showed us a small, private room where we could go to tell Angela goodbye. Immediately I plopped down in the nice rocking chair, because I was feeling really light-headed. I was afraid I was going to pass out. Mom sat in the other chair, and the nurse told us she would bring Angela to us in just a minute. So here we sit, waiting once again - this time with hearts breaking and tears flowing because we are going to tell Angela goodbye. How can a "bye" ever be "good"?

9:15 AM

Our ride is coming in a few minutes so we need to leave soon. I have been holding Angela for the past hour. She was wrapped up in a small blanket, and she had a tiny, little cap on her head. The nurse told us we could unwrap her, talk to her, sing to her - anything that would make her feel good. She said she was not in any pain, which made me relax a little. She then left us alone but said we could push a button if we needed any help.

At first, I just held her and rocked her, telling her how much I loved her. I kept repeating over and over again, "I'm so sorry, little girl, I'm so sorry." I felt that somehow this was all my fault. Angela was making the softest little squeaks with her voice, like she was trying to talk to me. At least, that was what I imagined.

Finally, I got brave and unwrapped her. She was so tiny; the nurse told me Angela weighed only 14 ounces, not even a pound, but I was so amazed at everything about her! She was perfectly formed, 10 fingers and toes – with the teeniest, tiniest little fingernails and toenails I could ever imagine. Her eyelids were still fused so I did not get to see her eyes. I hated that, but the nurse later told me that her eyes were being protected at this stage of her development.

I could tell she was struggling to breathe; her little lungs just were not developed enough yet. I then wrapped her back in the blanket so she would not get cold, and asked Mom if she wanted to hold her. Mom said she was too afraid, so I just kept rocking Angela, holding her to my chest and singing the lullabies I would have sung to her if I had been able to take her home with me.

It was a sweet time with my baby girl, and it was very painful to leave her. I still had hopes that she could live. Sadly, I got the idea from the NICU nurses that I could not stay and hold her until she passed away. So, I finally buzzed for the nurse to come and take her away. Mom and I went downstairs to wait for Loretta to come pick us up. Of course, they made me ride down in a wheelchair, which made me mad. I was not sick – just sick at heart.

Angela: "As Mom said, my lungs just are not yet fully developed because I am only 23 weeks gestationally, so it is hard to breathe. My lungs do not produce surfactant yet, a substance that is necessary for normal lung expansion. Most of my body is functioning well, but both my lungs and my digestive system are still very immature. Weighing less than a pound, the doctors did not think I would survive more than a few minutes.

My time with my mom was very special. I loved hearing her sing to me, and being held and rocked for the first time felt so lovely. Unfortunately, it would be the last time I would see my mother this side of heaven. That made both of us very sad."

—m—

Going Home

SATURDAY, MARCH 15TH, 10:30 AM

Mom and I were met at the front door by Amy, Andrew, and Grandma Jessie. I was trying so hard to be brave, as I leaned down to hug my children. I could not let them go, because my heart was breaking for all of us. To have a baby and not come home with her (or him) is one of the worst experiences I can imagine. This is indeed a very sad day…

"Amy, Andrew, your little sister has been born. She is still alive, but the doctors tell me that she is just too tiny, too premature, which means "born early," to live. Her lungs are not developed enough for her to breathe properly. I am so sorry. We can pray for her to have a peaceful time going up to see Jesus. Sadly, we do not always get a miracle, even though we pray very hard for one."

Before I could even close the front door, I heard the sweetest prayers for Angela coming out of the mouths of my children, and my tears flowed once again. After they finished, I began to tell them all about their baby sister - her weight, her dark hair, her teeny-tiny fingernails and toenails. I said I got to hold her for over an hour, and she made the quietest little squeaks, almost like she was talking to me.

I shared with them that I told Angela all about her older sister and brother that one day she would meet in heaven. Then I said that I needed to rest for a while, so the next thing I knew, I had two children lying right beside me in bed. As I was lying there with my kids, I began to wonder if I should take them up to see their baby sister. The more I thought about it, I was afraid that it would be too traumatic for them, especially if she was dead or died while they were holding her. Also, it was hard for me at first to look at someone so teeny-tiny, and I was afraid that if they saw her, it might haunt them for years to come.

12:15 PM

I must have fallen asleep because the next thing I remember is Mom coming to my bedroom door to see if I would come and eat a little lunch. She knew that I had not eaten anything today. It took a second to remember that I was no longer on bedrest, and to not check the status of my discharge when I went to pee. It still had not sunk in that none of that mattered anymore, because Angela had been born.

The first thing I did was call the hospital to see if Angela was still alive, which she was. Her nurse told me they were all really surprised that she was still with us. At that point, I began to question whether or not we should be doing something for her to keep her alive. It seemed to me that Angela wanted to live. The nurse tried to reassure me and answer my questions, but I was not satisfied. She told me she would have one of the neonatal doctors call me to discuss everything with me.

At lunch, Mom told me she had called Dad while I was asleep. She said he is on his way here to be with us. It will be quite a while, since my folks live 6 hrs. away. I need to see my dad. He will hold me in his arms, like he did when I was a child and needed to be comforted. I have been blessed with the best parents. I love them so much! And they love me...

1:30 PM

I am so sad. I just got off the phone with one of the neonatologists at the hospital. He basically told me that Angela was just too small and too premature to save.

He said, "She weighs less than a pound and her lungs are not developed enough for her to live."

He explained that anything they could do for her, such as starting an IV or putting her on a ventilator would maybe extend her life for a few hours, but they would only cause her pain. In the end, she would still die.

"Why is she still alive then?" I asked him. "Everyone told me she would live only a few minutes, and she's still alive. It has been almost 10 hours. She must want to live," I added.

Then he told me that because I was on bedrest for so long, with spotting and eventually contractions, that my body was probably secreting stress hormones that were being transferred to her through my placenta. That may have developed her lungs more than what was normally expected at 23-weeks' gestation. But it was not enough to save her. He said the little sounds she was making were from her struggle to breathe with only partially developed lungs. He said she did not yet have surfactant, a substance that helps the lungs to inflate as they should. He said that babies' bodies did not produce that until they were 26 weeks along.

After I hung up, all I could do was weep. When I got myself together as much as I could, I tried to explain to Mom and the kids what the doctor told me. Then we all wept together. I am trying to be strong for the kids, but I am not doing such a great job of it.

5:00 PM

I know Angela's nurse is tired of me calling her. I cannot help myself. I guess I still have hope despite the great odds. And she is still alive as of this time.

"Oh, please, Lord! A miracle? Please, please, please!"

5:40 PM

Angela Joy went to heaven after almost 14 hours of living. The nurse just called me. She told me no one expected her to live that long. Once again, I questioned whether we should have done more to help her to live. (I did not know then that this was something that would haunt me again and again for the next few years. The "what-ifs" would come at night when I could not get to sleep.)

When I told the kids that Angela had gone to heaven to see Jesus, they seemed to take it reasonably well. I think it is because I had prepared them for this all afternoon. Still, the tears flowed, as to be expected.

After I got myself more together, I called Harland to tell him our baby had died. He told me he was sorry, but I think he was probably just relieved.

6:00 PM

The doorbell just rang. I wonder who is here. Maybe it's Dad. It is! I fall into his arms, weeping, and tell him that Angela just died 20 minutes ago. He told me he loves me, and how sorry he is that this has happened to me. He held me tightly, as we cried together. Then of course, he hugged mom and the kids, and we all got in the biggest group hug we could make.

SUNDAY, MARCH 16, 12:05 AM

I just cannot get to sleep. I think I am still in shock with everything that has happened. All I can do is weep…and I am doing it so very quietly into my pillow because I do not want my children to hear me. I find no comfort in God, although I continue to pray…

"Where are you, Lord? Don't you hear my heart breaking? Why don't I feel your arms around me? Where is your comfort now, when I need it the most? Why did you let her die? You know I wanted her. Now, I will never see that little girl going off to kindergarten like I imagined so vividly! I am so angry with you, God! I know you could have saved her! Why didn't you?"

—∞—

No Time to Grieve

MONDAY, MARCH 17, 1986

I do not know how much sleep I have been able to get in the past 2 nights. If I do sleep a little, every time I wake up, the reality just hits me again like a punch in the gut. It is like living the nightmare over and over and over again.

My family have all been so very loving, and I am trying my best to keep it together for them. None of us went to church yesterday. Even though very few people there knew about my pregnancy, I just could not face anybody and pretend like everything was fine.

Today I got a call from Gary Buell from Buell's Chapel. Apparently, I had never signed the papers regarding what to do with Angela's body. Things were happening so fast in the hospital that I failed to sign anything. And I thank God that I had not. My son, Andrew, was strongly against cremating Angela, and I was afraid that it might be too late. In fact, I had already bought a beautiful pink little box in which to keep her remains. But now I had the option of burying her. And that is what I told him I wanted to do. So, we arranged for me to go to the cemetery with him tomorrow to pick out a spot to bury Angela. We talked about the option of having a graveside service for her.

As soon as we got off the phone, I started making plans that in some ways made the reality of Angela's death a little less consuming of my every thought and action. I know that sounds weird, but I think I am still in a state of shock. Somehow you do the things you have to do, but it feels like it is happening to someone else.

I got on the phone with my younger brother, Rick, and he agreed to build her a little casket, despite the fact that he was already struggling with depression at this time. I prayed that it would not make things worse for him. He is so kind to do this for me.

My good friend, Carlene, told me she would make Angela a dress and bonnet from a doll pattern she had. I was able to find some fabric that had tiny, little pink roses on it. I even found matching quilted fabric that I would be able to use to line the casket.

My older brother, Rod, (the pastor) said that he would send me some materials he had from when he had conducted funerals for babies. Of course, I asked him if he would do the service for Angela. I knew I would not be able to get through it. He felt honored to do it. You do not think about the sad things that pastors have to do as they shepherd their flock... until that day that it involves you. Bless him!

Next, I was able to talk with some of the people in my Praise Messenger group. They were all willing to come and sing at the service. My thoughts turned to what I would like for them to sing. So, things began to quickly fall into place, despite the sadness that now surrounded me. Sadness is such a consuming emotion.

Somehow, when we are having to plan a funeral, especially an unexpected one, we go into "shock-mode." We do what we must do, but we do not let ourselves feel what we are doing. We have no time for emotions; we turn into "task robots," as though someone else has taken over our body, and we are void of feelings...

...until night comes...and with it, comes reality. Reality returns our emotions to us like a gut punch! It is so hard not to relive everything that has happened in the past 5½ months – the shock of the pregnancy, the difficult decision, the dread and embarrassment of telling my boyfriend, my friends, my children, and my parents...Angela's birth...her death...

I keep thinking, "Why? Why, Lord? Why?" And He never answers me... At least I never hear Him...

—m—

BabyLand

TUESDAY, MARCH 18, 1986

Today was a horrible day – from start to finish! First, my milk started coming in – big time…literally! My breasts got as hard as a rock, and they began to hurt so much. Thank heavens the nurse had warned me that the shot she gave me did not always work. I would not have expected this. Let me tell you, there is nothing sadder than having your body produce milk and having no baby to feed. It is like an "in your face" betrayal. "Your baby died, Renée! Just in case you forgot you had one."

After we got the kids off to school, I called Dr. York's office and asked if there was anything I could do to decrease the pain. One thing I had already done that morning when I first woke up was to take a hot shower, where I tried to express some milk so my breasts would not be so painful. That was the exact opposite of what I should have done. The nurse suggested cold compresses, taking Tylenol, and avoiding touching or stimulating my nipples. She also suggested putting cold cabbage in my bra – really? - but I had to meet the funeral director this morning, so that definitely was not going to work. Mom said that they used to tightly wrap folded towels around the breast area. Maybe we can try that tonight.

After starting the morning so awfully, I thought nothing could get worse. Then I saw the saddest thing I have ever seen in my whole life. I went with Gary Buell to Rest Haven Memorial Park (how can they call it a park?) to pick out a gravesite for Angela. Mr. Buell had already informed me that there was a section of the cemetery devoted just to babies called BabyLand. But what broke my heart was walking through it, seeing grave after grave, row after row of baby tombstones (grave markers). So many of them…how could this many families survive what I was now walking…or should I say, "stumbling" …through?

"God, how can this be? So much pain represented here…I just do not understand."

I suppose the tremendous number of baby deaths should have brought me some comfort in knowing I was not alone, but all I could do was weep! Weep for my own child, and weep for all those families who have suffered such great pain. And so many twins were buried there. It was just too much for my broken spirit to deal with.

Finally, when I had composed myself, I chose a spot for Angela, signed some papers, and then Mr. Buell took me home. He is such a loving and kind man. I do not envy his job. How does he deal with people's sorrows, day after day? Especially when it involves the death of a baby?

"God, please bless this man for what he does."

By the time I got home, my bra was wet from my breasts leaking. You see, every time I thought of Angela while in BabyLand, I would get that "let-down" feeling that you would normally get right before you go to nurse your baby. Having nursed both Amy and Andrew, I knew exactly what was happening to me. And every time it did happen, it was another "gut punch" reminder that my baby was gone!

Trying to sleep tonight was a futile endeavor, as images of grave after grave of lost infants filled my mind and fractured my heart. And of course, my painful, full breasts reminded me that my baby would soon be joining them there in BabyLand.

—◊—

The Graveside Service

FRIDAY, MARCH 21, 1986

It has almost been one week since Angela was born, and it has been the craziest few days ever! So much to do but God has made it all come together for tomorrow's graveside service for Angela Joy. Yet, I find I am completely numb. Foolishly, I am still in the habit of checking the color of my discharge when I pee. Then reality hits me in the gut like a fist, as I remember my baby died. That sounds foolish, but I think I am still in a "grief fog." At least my milk is finally beginning to dry up, although there are still times I find the front of my blouse wet. I am still having to wear pads in my bra because of that.

Dad went back home for a few days so he could bring back the little casket my brother Rick has made for Angela. To keep myself occupied, I focused on planning her graveside service. I was worried that a week was too long to wait to bury her after she died, but when I called the funeral director, he explained that when a baby as small as Angela dies, they cannot put embalming fluid in their tiny veins. Instead, they immerse them in it. I hated that picture in my mind, but it was better than the much worse picture I had been envisioning.

Dad got back into town on Thursday, and brought the beautiful casket Rick had made. When I saw the size of it, it broke my heart all over again. I was able to line it with the quilted rosebud fabric I found. It turned out perfect except for all the tears that flowed down as I worked to secure the fabric in it.

I experienced that same grief when my friend Carline brought over the cap and gown she had made from the doll pattern. Again, they were so, so tiny, but beautiful. Although I know Angela is in heaven, it feels good that she will be buried with such love.

Earlier this week, I got the info re: an infant's funeral service from my brother, Rod. I have been rewriting it a bit so it would say just what I want it to say. I have chosen two songs for the Praise Messengers to sing, so everything is falling into place. I still hate this, though...

This afternoon, I took the casket and clothes to the funeral parlor. I was offered a chance to wait and see her dressed, and in the casket, but I just could not do it. As kind as Mr. Buell was, I had to get out of there. It was too sad...

I know Angela is in the arms of Jesus, but I wish I could feel His arms around me. I feel so alone in my grief. I know I am still angry at God for not letting Angela live. The nights are the worst because I have no distractions, and all I think about is "*Why?* Why did she have to die?" My tears dry on my cheeks when exhaustion finally allows me to sleep.

SATURDAY, MARCH 22, 1986, 8:00 AM

Today is Angela's graveside service up at the cemetery. There will be just a few people there because not that many people even know that I was pregnant. Of course, Mom and Dad are here. My brother Rod is doing the service for me, but his wife, Toni, had to stay home with their children. My younger brother Rick and his family are unable to come. Rick is still struggling with depression, so I totally understand. I also asked our "adopted" grandparents, George and Jessie Lindley to come, and they are planning on being there. Although I told Harland about the graveside service, he is choosing not to come. I am not surprised, but it still hurts. Most of the Praise Messengers will be there because they are singing. A couple of other friends may be coming, but like I said, most of my friends are not even aware of what is going on. I am praying that I will be strong for my children.

9:00 AM

When we arrived at the cemetery, there was such a stillness in the air as my family and friends gave my children and me hugs and quiet words of condolence. When I first saw the casket, even though there was a beautiful spray of pink roses upon it, my heart was stricken with pain anew as I saw its tiny size.

"Why, God? Why? It just is not right to have to bury a baby! She was my baby! Why did you take her?" But I heard no answer from heaven.

The following is the service we had for Angela:

OPENING SCRIPTURE READING:
> "You have set your glory above the heavens. From the lips of children and infants you have ordained praise."
> Psalm 8:1-2a

PRAYER: (BY RODNEY)

SONG: (BY PRAISE MESSENGERS) "I LOVE YOU, LORD!"

EULOGY:
Angela Joy was born on March 15, 1986, in Eugene, Oregon, at 3:42 AM. She weighed 14 ounces and was 10 inches long. She lived for only 14 short hours, and died at 5:40 PM, March 15th. She is survived by her mother, Renée; her father, Harland; her sister, Amy; her brothers, Andrew, and Javan, Kael, and Jenner. She is also survived by both her maternal and paternal grandparents, and several aunts, uncles, and cousins. We are here today to remember Angela Joy with love, and to commit her spirit into the hands of Jesus.

OLD TESTAMENT SCRIPTURE:

Excerpts from Psalm 139

"O, Lord, Thou has searched me and known me.

Thou dost know when I sit down and when I rise up.

Thou dost understand my thoughts from afar.

Thou dost scrutinize my path and my lying down,

And art intimately acquainted with all my ways…

Thou has enclosed me behind and before,

And laid Thy hand upon me.

Such knowledge is too wonderful for me;

It is too high; I cannot attain to it…

For Thou didst form my inward parts;

Thou didst weave me in my mother's womb.

I will give thanks to Thee, for I am fearfully and wonderfully made;

Wonderful are Thy works,

And my soul knows it very well.

My frame was not hidden from Thee,

When I was made in secret,

And skillfully wrought in the depths of the earth.

Thine eyes have seen my unformed substance;

And in Thy book, they were all written,

The days that were ordained for me,

When as yet there was not one of them.

How precious also are Thy thoughts to me, O God.

How vast is the sum of them!

If I should count them, they would outnumber the sand.

When I awake, I am still with Thee." KJV

NEW TESTAMENT SCRIPTURE:

"And Jesus said, 'Let the children come to me…for the kingdom of heaven belongs to such as these." Matthew 19:14

MESSAGE:

We have gathered here today to offer our comfort, support, and love. We want to express our sympathy to the family and friends in the passing of Angela Joy. We turn to God for His Divine strength in this time of sorrow. We remember the words in Philippians 4:13 NKJV: "**I can do all things through Christ who strengthens me...**"

Even though Angela Joy only lived a short time, she was a special child of God. She will always hold a special place in Renée's and Harland's hearts, and will be remembered with love by Amy, Andrew, and their families and friends. We know that Renée gave Angela the spirit to want to survive. As tiny as she was, she lived much longer than expected – she was a real fighter! I also believe she sensed the precious love expressed by her mother, as she held her and rocked her while she was still alive. Love is a real gift that we can all give to one another, both in times of joy and times of sorrow. And we are thankful for God's love shown to us in the giving of His Son Jesus.

Angela will NOT be forgotten. God will take care of her now, as she lives with Him and His angels in heaven.

In the most beautiful gardens, though carefully tended by the most skillful botanist, there is an occasional rose that buds, but never opens. In all respects the rose is like all the others, but some unseen cause keeps it from blooming. It wilts and fades away without coming to its radiant unfolding.

What happens in nature's garden occasionally happens also in the garden of God's human family. A baby is born – beautiful, precious – but with some unseen hand sealing that life so that it can never come to its rightful unfolding. This child, too, like the bud that never fully opens, faded away to be gathered back into God's heavenly garden of souls. We do not understand why, but we accept God's will and infinite wisdom.

COMMITTAL:
Confident in our resurrection and the almighty power of God, we now commit this infant into God's loving arms and care. Angela Joy, you are now our Angel of Joy! We shall miss you!

SONG: (BY PRAISE MESSENGERS) "IN HIS TIME"
Maranatha Music
(Renée, Amy, Andrew, Grandma and Grandpa [in turn] place rosebud on casket.)

BENEDICTION:
Now may you **"Trust in the Lord with all your heart, and lean not on your own understanding. In all your ways acknowledge Him, and He will direct your paths."** (Proverbs 3:5-6 NKJV)

In Jesus' Holy and Precious name, AMEN

After the service ended and the hugs were given, people drifted away to their cars. My 9-yr old son, Andrew, decided he wanted to see Angela in her casket. I was afraid of what she might look like after a week, and I did not want him to remember her that way. I knew that she now wore the little doll dress and bonnet that my friend Carline made for her, but I had not seen her at the funeral home since she died, so I just did not know what to do.

One of my regrets is that I did not take my children up to see her at the hospital and let them hold her before she died. I believe it would have brought a better closure for them. After all, they had lost a little sister.

In the end, I did not open the casket for my son...out of fear. So, we had to say our final goodbyes to Angela Joy at the cemetery. It was so difficult to leave her there in BabyLand. Although I knew she was in the arms of Jesus in heaven, still my heart was breaking.

Angela's gravestone

Casket made by
my brother, Rick.

Doll bonnet and gown
made by my friend, Carline

Letters of Sympathy

Because I lost Angela at five months, most of the people in my life did not even know I was pregnant. So, it was only the few friends and family I told who sent me letters of sympathy. Here are three special ones:

Dear Renée and family,

Just know that our prayers are with all of you today.

Renée, our Lord won't give us more than we can handle but at times like this, one finds it hard not to question that!

Angela Joy's time with you was so short but remember her as one of God's gifts, and your experience with her has made you all the stronger. I already have been in awe of your strength and courage over the years. You are truly an inspiration to me and anyone else who knows you.

I pray that time will bring you comfort and understanding, and I know the Lord has good times in store for you.

Love, Connie

Connie has always been a friend who knows just the right things to say to make me feel better. God bless her!

"Lord, I remember how hard it was to tell my parents about Angela, and now I realize that they were grieving for and with me." Mom quietly handed me these letters the day after Angela's graveside service:

March 21, 1986

Enclosed is a little love gift to help with funeral expenses.

This last month has meant a great deal to me in many ways. Being with you and seeing how much you wanted Angela Joy has really helped me accept your pregnancy, and seeing Angela made me know I would have loved and cherished her as much as any of my grandchildren.

As so many of your friends have said, "You are a brave young woman" and I will continue to pray that someday you will find the happiness and fulfillment you deserve.

We have shared so much that I feel closer to you than I have for a long time.

I love you,
Mom

My dearest Renée:

I love you so much and feel for you as you go through this most trying time of your life. We know that Angela is singing with the cherubs today in Heaven and some day we will all join her.

I know that someday you will find someone worthy of your love, and that love and companionship will be yours. In the meanwhile, your love of God and Christ will sustain you. Your faith is so strong and you are a wonderful daughter to me.

We pray constantly for your happiness and peace of mind. You've come a long way in acceptance of life's tragedies but your faith will help you through it all as you continue to put your life in God's hands.

Remember that as long as we are alive and have our faculties, we will be there to help you and your kids through anything that comes.

Love you as long as I have breath,

Dad

Several other people sent sweet cards offering their support for the kids and me. Others sent flowers. One friend bought me a pink rosebush to plant in my yard as a remembrance of Angela. Those who knew about her, loved on us as best they could. Yet, the tears still come, especially at night when no one can see.

"Do You see me, Lord?"

"Where are You, God?"

MARCH 30, 1986

It's been over a week since we had Angela's funeral, and now is the time for the healing to begin. The problem is that my healing is nowhere to be found. I cry myself to sleep night after night, begging for God to put His arms around me. But I cannot feel His comfort, or His arms. It is as though He has deserted me. In all honesty, I blame Him for not saving my Angela. Everything in my soul believes that He had the power to do it, but He choose to let her die.

"God, I am so angry with you! Where are you when I need you the most? I don't understand why I had to go through the humiliation of telling my kids, my parents, my brothers, my fellow nurses, a few close friends...and then, just as I accept this whole pregnancy and am even looking forward to it, You let her die! Why? Why? Why? I just do not understand..."

I am doing my best to hide my pain from my children. As parents, we never want to let our children see us emotionally upset. We do not want to disturb them; we want to protect them. So, during the morning I fake great strength until they catch the school bus, and then I resolve to dry my tears and be cheerful when they come home from school. But my heart is broken, and I do not know if it can ever be mended again. My nights are the worst, as I reach out to God and cannot feel Him, so I cry myself to sleep – alone once again in my grief.

―⁓―

Back to Church and Work

MARCH 31, 1986

The hospital was generous with my bereavement pay. They gave me five paid days, which extended to two weeks' time because of my part-time status. After all my time in bed, I only lost two days of pay, which was a true blessing. But because I had used up all my sick leave, vacation leave, and personal leave when I was on bedrest for so long, I needed to go back to work today. It. Was. Horrible!

As I walked into my unit at the hospital, it felt like all eyes were on me. Not one, no, not one person said, "I'm sorry for your loss." Doesn't anybody care? I cannot help but wonder if they think I am glad I lost her because I am not married. Finally, one friend gave me a hug. But it was as though it never happened. But it *did*! It *did* happen! I know people don't always know what to say when a child dies, but at least they could say, "I'm sorry".

Once again, my heart literally hurts inside me, and my eyes betray me with those tears I must wipe away before I get back home to Amy and Andrew.

Yesterday was Easter Sunday. I somehow managed to make myself get up, get the kids motivated to get ready, and we all walked into church as though nothing had happened. I shed a few tears, but Easter is an acceptable time to cry because of what Jesus did on the cross for us. So no one thought twice about my tears, except for my friend Carline, the one who made Angela her burial clothes, and who was kind enough to sit with me and squeeze my hand when I needed it.

At church, only a handful of people know that I am grieving - the Praise Messengers ensemble group and two or three other friends. Once again, I pretend that all is well. Sometimes I wonder how many other people there are grieving, or upset, or hurt…and yet we pretend that all is well. We hide behind our masks of deception.

Sometimes, though, it is "proper" to show our emotions in church. As a body of believers, we all grieve and express our sympathy when someone loses a spouse, or a parent, or even worse, a child. It's just that my child was a secret. Even one of the few friends I had shared with about Angela, my friend Mary, asked me why I had a funeral service for a "miscarriage." Wow! I was not expecting that. I was left speechless…

Easter is a time to celebrate the resurrection of Jesus Christ from the grave. He is my only hope of ever seeing Angela again. He gave us eternal life when He defeated death on the cross. I know Jesus loved me enough to die for me, yet I still cannot seem to find Him in those dark, lonely hours at night. In my heart, I know He is there with me, but I do not feel Him. Not now, at least… perhaps it is because I am so angry at Him for allowing Angela to die. I know He could have saved her. Why didn't He?

I also blame myself. What did I do that caused this? Was it all the stress I experienced during this pregnancy? Was it because of my sin? My nights in bed are filled with questions… and tears…

Romans 8:28 in the Bible says: **"And we know that in all things God works for the good of those who love Him, who have been called according to His purpose."**

I know God always has a plan and a purpose for all that happens, but I still can not see how this could ever lead to anything "good" for me. And I do love Him, even though I am angry with Him. And honestly, I am having a hard time wondering what His purpose could possibly be for all of this.

"When, Lord? When?"

APRIL 15, 1986

It has been one month since Angela died. I wish I could say I am doing better, but I am not. I have not heard a word from Harland. I guess Angela's death was a relief to him. But for me, every morning I still wake up and wish her death had been only a bad dream. Don't get me wrong: I love my other two children dearly, but I still miss the one who could be having breakfast with us. Actually, she would not be. She would still be in my womb developing into a beautiful little girl. Her full-term due date was not until July 15th.

One of the saddest things I have had to do this past month was to return things I had bought or borrowed because of this pregnancy. First, it was the maternity clothes I borrowed from the various girls in the "Praise Messengers" group. The maternity clothes I had bought for myself ended up stuffed in a bag to donate to whoever.

The hardest experience I had was when I took the extra sheet set I had bought for Angela, so that she and Amy would have matching sheets someday. A someday that would never come. The saleslady wanted to know the reason I was returning them. When I cried and told her my baby died and would never need them, I think I ruined her day.

One thing I kept, which was probably foolish, was the little clown that matched the sheets. Sometimes when I am very sad, I turn his nose and listen to the sweet melody I had hoped to play for Angela one day. Again, a day that would never come.

When Angela died, the hospital gave me a little "Death Packet" with information about various organizations to help people who are grieving.

The Lord knows someone needs to help me. So, the other night I got a babysitter and went to a Compassionate Friends meeting. Compassionate Friends is especially for parents who have lost a child. It was similar to what I imagine Alcoholics' Anonymous is like. You tell your name, and then you tell your story. You don't have to share if you don't want to. I did not. But I cried with every single family who did share.

A beautiful young couple runs this local CF, and of course they, too, had lost a child. It was such a sad meeting, but I think it did me some good to cry, and to realize that I am not the only one who bears such a heavy burden. Maybe I will share my story the next time I go. It might make me feel better.

Sadly, about a month after Angela died, a 2-year-old boy with leukemia, Kyle, passed away. His parents were a young couple in our church, and all of us had been praying for Kyle for months. For me, it was living Angela's death all over again.

Although it was very hard for me, I attended Kyle's funeral since I knew his parents so well. His daddy wrote the most beautiful poem to him. It broke my heart, and my tears flowed once again. His parents had no idea that my tears were also for the loss of my little girl. Yes, I cried for Kyle's parents because I understood their great pain, but my tears were also for me. And a part of me wished that my church family could have known about Angela, for I feel so desperate as I grieve alone.

I know one thing - I am nothing like David in that sermon I heard! I cannot just get up, clean up, change my clothes, and go and worship God. Sometimes I feel I will never again have an appetite, care about my appearance, take off my "mourning clothes," and truly worship God again.

"Lord, I know I am still angry with You because You took Angela away from me, but I beg You to answer these questions: 'Why must I grieve alone? When will I ever feel Your arms around me again? When, Lord? When?'"

APRIL 24, 1986

Last night I went to another Compassionate Friends meeting. I had decided before the meeting that I would share my story with everyone. As I looked across the table, to my surprise, there sat Kyle's parents. Wow! They were some of my church friends who did not know I had just lost a baby. Could I really let them in on my secret? Could I trust them? Still, I felt the Holy Spirit nudging me to tell my story. So I did…tearfully, of course. I revealed that I was unmarried at the time, but I did not mention that my loss was recent. Then they shared their story about Kyle, which made all of us cry again, especially me.

Sure enough, they came up to me afterwards, gave me a hug, and thanked me for sharing. Of course, I expressed my sympathy to them. As we talked about our great losses, they asked me if mine was when I was a teenager. Gulp! I did not want to lie, so I took a chance, and answered them honestly, saying: "It was last month." There was definitely a look of surprise on their faces, but I did not see condemnation. Then we hugged again and cried together.

"Lord Jesus, thank You for answering my desire that my church people would know about Angela. You sent me Kyle's parents. Not only do they know about my great grief, they totally understand the pain that comes from losing a child. We will be there for each other now."

—⁓—

Sorrow-Hope-Sorrow-Hope

SUNDAY, APRIL 27, 1986 – FROM SORROW TO HOPE

I am at a very low point today, especially after church this morning. Everyone was so sad because of Kyle's death. It has really affected me, as it brought up so many issues that I have been struggling with. Once again, it is "Why?"

I realize that I do not feel like doing anything except having a pity party for myself. Even the few people who know about Angela do not seem to understand why I am still grieving. Just the other day at work, one of my good friends there asked me why I could not "get over it," as though there was a timeline when you should stop grieving a dead child.

"Lord, I am not even sure You understand. When I cry alone at night, I do not feel You there at all. You are the One who took her. I feel like I am grieving alone."

After a couple of hours, my pity party got tiresome with only me, myself, and I attending. I have decided to get a babysitter for the kids tonight, and go to Faith Center, a huge church where nobody knows me, and I can just blend into the crowd. I just need to get away from the sadness I feel. Also, I need some spiritual rejuvenation. I do not want my sadness to affect Amy and Andrew.

—⁂—

Wow! I cannot believe what happened tonight! I got there early so only a few people were scattered around the large sanctuary. My plan was to sit hidden in the back row. Then I looked at the front of the sanctuary and there sat my former Avon lady with her husband. I had not seen them in several years because we moved to a different neighborhood, but I just had to go say "Hello" to them. She and I had gotten quite close, despite me being "a customer." I was a newlywed at the time and she was a few years older, so she used to give me advice about marriage. (Apparently, it did not work for me.) But it was a sweet reunion, and I told them about my kids, my divorce, going to nursing school, etc.

And the next thing I knew, I started sharing everything about Angela and her death. Of course, I was still very emotional and shed more than a few tears. They were very loving and nonjudgmental as they listened. They even cried with me a little. Then they told me that this church had a few counseling services that anyone could use if needed. They even said they knew of "the perfect counselor" for me.

I thought about it all during the church service, and I really felt the Holy Spirit telling me this was what I needed to do. So, after church, I told them I would like to do this. They took my phone number and said they would arrange it. Someone would call me to set up a time.

"Lord, I know You orchestrated all of this. First, I never go to this church, nor am I ever early for anything. And I had not seen my Avon lady in over 10 years, yet she remembered me when I approached her. I did not plan on sharing anything with her and her husband, but it all came pouring out of me. Thank You, Lord, for giving me some hope that I might begin to heal from everything that has happened."

THURSDAY, MAY 1, 1986, 11:30 AM – MORE HOPE

Last Tuesday, I got a call from the counseling service at Faith Center. I could not believe they called me so soon! I know my friends must have told them I was desperate. So, this morning I met with a kind, loving counselor...her name is Wanda. She is a few years older than I am and seems to have a lot of wisdom. Before I shared anything, she prayed with me. Then she asked me why I was there.

Maybe because she was a stranger…or perhaps it was the kindness I saw in her eyes…or the Kleenex box that she had ready for me…whatever it was, I easily opened up to her. When I finished sharing my story…many tears later… she asked me if she could share something with me. Of course, I said "Yes."

Then she proceeded to tell me that she had a 16-yr old daughter who just had a baby born out of wedlock. Her daughter and the baby were living at home with Wanda and her husband. My first thought was why did that baby live, and why did mine have to die? (Of course, I did not verbalize that thought…but I sure thought it.)

Wanda went on to say that she understood a lot of what I shared with her…except it was from a parent's perspective. She also said that what I shared was something she needed to hear to give her a better understanding of what her daughter had been going through. In other words, she wanted me to know that she and I would be good for each other. She too felt that God orchestrated my surprise reunion with my Avon lady, and then He brought Wanda and me together. Her sharing her story made me feel a lot closer to her, especially since it was only my first session with her. After we talked a little more, she prayed with me, and then we set another appointment for May 20th.

Afterwards, I began to have a little hope that I could survive this all-consuming grief that was crushing me with its heavy hands.

"Thank You, Lord, for bringing Wanda into my life. I should never forget that You are still in control and You always want the best for my life. It is so hard to remember that when we are in the midst of our grief. Thanks for hope, Jesus. Help me remember that You are my Hope."

MAY 1, 1986, 3:30 PM – BACK TO SORROW

I just had my 7-wk follow-up, postpartum appointment with Dr. York. Sitting in the waiting room and seeing several obviously pregnant ladies there with me was very depressing. When I was finally put in a room, got undressed, put on the horrible skimpy gown all women love, and sat there waiting for Dr. York to come in, I totally lost it. I could not stop crying for my sweet Angela. As I sat there bawling my eyes out, I remembered how just a few months ago I sat here crying desperately because I was pregnant. What irony that it would come to this!

When Dr. York and the nurse came in, it was obvious that I had been weeping…actually, I still was. After I got myself together a little, Dr. York took my hands in his and tried to reassure me that everything was going to be alright. Once he examined me, told me everything looked good, it was my turn to ask him my list of questions:

Why? ("We don't know. We may never know.")

Did it have to do with my placenta? ("There was a small tear on the edge that probably was the source of the bleeding. Your uterus got irritable, but we don't know for sure why it did.")

Was it because I took the CVS test? (Possibly, but it probably would have happened sooner.)

Was it related to my stress? ("Possibly, but we don't know.")

Was it her heart? ("All indications on ultrasound showed it was good. Plus, she lived much longer than we anticipated. She had a strong heart.")

Was it because I played volleyball once a week? ("Exercise is good for pregnant women. Plus, you were on bedrest for most of the month before she was born.")

Was it my fault? ("No, Renée. We just will probably never know why this happened.")

When I left the doctor's office, I felt like I got no real answers – except for a bunch of "We don't knows" - and that was not what I wanted to hear. Without any definitive answers, I was back to blaming God and myself.

MAY 6, 1986 – HOPE…OR SORROW?

I received a letter today from Mom, and she enclosed a letter written to her and Dad. It was from one of my older cousins, Pat. Part of it said this:

Dear Aunt Marge and Uncle Rod,

I've been praying a lot for you lately. Mom told me about Renée, and I've really been praying for her too. I remember when she was born, and the first picture I ever saw of her.

She is very blessed to have a mom and dad as kind and loving as you. I know she really loves you a lot – and telling you what happened was probably one of the hardest things she's ever had to do. We don't want to disappoint our parents – and knowing they still love us – and forgive us – is a true gift from God. Not all girls have this – (I'm thankful I do.)

I know God has been helping her – and loving her. One of my first thoughts was, she is going to be so much more understanding and kind – and it can't help but make her a more compassionate nurse – and friend – and woman. I think God takes our biggest mistakes and turns them around to somehow make us stronger and more of a blessing to others.

I can't tell you how much I admire her for not getting an abortion – that took a lot of determination, I'm sure. Especially when so many wouldn't have hesitated.

I don't expect what I'm saying to help any – I know you have probably already thought of all these things. I just needed to write – and share – and tell you I love you – and I'm thankful I'm part of your family and that you are part of mine."

With love and prayers,

Pat

They were sweet words that did encourage me...and made me cry, for once not because of grief, but because her words gave me hope. But right now, I am not sure I feel much understanding or compassion or love or strength or like a blessing to others...or like someone who should be admired by anyone. Right now, what I feel is dead... Let's face it – I am a sorrowful mess! My emotions are up and down - mostly down. Sometimes I feel like I am chained to a roller coaster that will never let me off.

MAY 20, 1986 – HOPE

Today I had another appointment with my grief counsellor, Wanda. It went fairly well, but there were still a lot of tears as I told her that my feelings were so erratic...one minute I would feel hopeful that I was going to break free of the grip that grief held on me, and the next I would be weeping again. She told me that was perfectly normal for someone who had been through what I had been through. She said that grieving takes time; you cannot rush it, no matter how much you would like to just be done with it.

Anyway, after I left, I was feeling more hopeful than I had been in a long time. Wanda told me she thought that we could just meet once a month for now. That also made me feel hopeful. So, we'll see...

A Sad Summer

JUNE 26, 1986

I started the month with an appointment with Wanda on the 3rd. It turned out to be a more difficult session than I expected. She asked me some tough questions, such as what was my relationship with God at this time. I really did not want to answer that question, because I knew I was still mad at Him. I admitted that I was not praying like I used to do.

Of course, at home the kids and I still took turns saying grace at our mealtimes, and at bedtime, I listened to their prayers as usual. But my own prayer life was not good. I was not sure I could trust God anymore. So why should I ask Him for anything or even talk to Him?

Wanda challenged me to at least start each new morning with a prayer to thank God for a new day. She reminded me that each day was a gift. Then at night, I was to thank Him for the day He had given me. She told me to find at least one good thing that happened that day to thank God for, and to keep a notebook to write it down. At the end of each week, I was to go back and read all the good things that the Lord had given me that week. I promised her I would try.

The rest of the month was all about Amy and Andrew. School had ended for the year, and they were both involved with summer league soccer, at least they will be until the time that they leave for Alaska to visit their dad for several weeks. I was still working 3-4 shifts a week at the hospital. Between that and the kids, I stayed busy, so I did not have to think about my sadness...at least during the day.

But it is the nights that are killing me. I still feel so alone at night. When all is quiet, I begin to think about Angela, and the fact that I would still be pregnant if I had not lost her. And then the "blame game" begins. I realize I am still mad at God, mad at myself, and mad at Harland, who I have not heard from even once since Angela died. I realize I am mad about everything that has happened in the last eight months. Not just mad…I am sad, and it is killing me!

I am keeping my promise to Wanda, and I do have a notebook of good things to thank God for, but that is about as far as my prayers go.

I am living, but I feel nothing except for "Blah." Blah about my life, blah about myself, blah, blah, blah! Wanda thinks I am depressed. Yes, I am! So now what?

JULY 2, 1986

Amy and Andrew have just left for Alaska to spend 5 weeks with their dad and step-mom. This is usually a bittersweet time for me. As a single parent, this is the only time (other than every other Christmas) that I am not responsible for taking care of my children 24/7. So, it is a relief…at first. Then after about a week, I really start missing the kids. And now, with the death of Angela, the house seems even more quiet. If she had not been born early, I would be 8½ months pregnant and looking forward to her arrival in 2 weeks. Instead, here I sit, alone except for the "what-ifs" to think about.

Thank heavens I still have my friends, my church, my part-time nursing job, and my Lord. I will probably pick up several extra shifts at work this summer to make some money without having to worry about a babysitter. Usually, I do something fun for myself when the kids are away, but this year I don't care about doing anything. The extra shifts at work will occupy my mind for 8-9 hours during the day. The extra money is nice too…maybe I can be like Uncle Scrooge and be happy counting my money.

JULY 4, 1986 – 11 PM

This was a sad day for me. Instead of celebrating today like most people, I spent my day working at the hospital…at least I was getting time and a half pay. And it was a long day today. But it is tonight that is hard.

Hearing the last of the fireworks in the distance, my tears are flowing once again, as I remember last year's 4th of July.

It was a year ago today that I met Harland after he had run in a 10-K race. I went to watch the annual 4th of July race because my kids had just left for Alaska, and I was lonely and bored, and half of the town came to watch. I just wanted to be around people. And I met him...

Harland ended up inviting me to go with him and his two oldest boys to the fireworks at the football stadium. That is how our dating life began. And now he is married to someone else. No wonder I feel so sad tonight about this day. I think about all that has happened in the past year. What if I had never met him? What if I had said "No" to the fireworks? What if I had never had Angela? What if she had not died? As I lie here in bed trying to sleep, I am plagued with the "What ifs?"

I saw my counselor, Wanda, on July 1st. That was only three days ago, and we talked about some hard days coming up this month, including today. But I think the worst day will be the 15th, which was Angela's predicted due date. I am not sure how I am going to get through that difficult day. Wanda thought I should do something special for myself, but I don't have any desire to do anything.

There was another difficult thing Wanda and I discussed on the 1st...the topic of forgiveness. This was my fourth session with Wanda. She thinks that I am making good progress, but she stressed the importance of forgiveness to me. She explained that forgiving someone, even when that Someone is God Himself, is a process. It takes time and it takes determination.

Forgiveness is a choice, and most times it is a very difficult choice, especially if there was deep hurt involved. She told me that before I could move on with my life, I needed to forgive anyone who had hurt me during this time. She explained that when people hold on to anger, the anger is actually hurting them. Anger begins to eat at your soul.

Then Wanda asked me to make a list - to write down people I needed to forgive. If I was angry with God, I was to include Him too. Hmm...she already knew that God would make my list. I *was* angry with God, and of course I thought I had the right to be angry. She asked me to pray about this and come back the next time with my list of who I needed to forgive.

Before I left, Wanda prayed for me. She asked God to open my heart so that I could truly feel His presence surrounding me this month, especially on the 15th, Angela's due date. I still do not have any idea of what to do on that day. Maybe I will take flowers to Angela's grave. That will be very hard to do, but I will be crying anyway, so why not share my heart with her.

JULY 20, 1986

I just got back from a 5-day trip up to Seattle to see my friends, Jim and Sally. They called and invited me to spend a few days with them. They knew about my due date, for Jim was the first person I called when I found out I was pregnant.

They have seven kids between them, so I knew that would keep my mind occupied. And Sally and I always have many, many laughs together. She has the same kind of humor as I do, and we get along great. And Jim has been a dear friend for many, many years.

So, after my visit to the cemetery, I spent Angela's due date on the road, and I had a lot of time to talk to the Lord. A lot of tears were shed along that 6-hr journey, both up there and back, but it was good for me. And my time with my friends was such a blessing. I am beginning to believe that perhaps I will survive this past year. There is hope on the horizon.

AUGUST 5, 1986

I just got back from picking up the kids at the Portland airport. They have been in Alaska the past five weeks. Oh, how much I have missed them! I was never so happy to have them back as I am today! An empty house is a lonely house. At least for me, this summer it sure was...

—⁂—

Learning to Forgive

AUGUST 12, 1986

Today at my counseling session, I was feeling pretty good because I only had three people on my "forgiveness" list – my friend Mary, my "boy-fiend" (I mean my boyfriend, Harland), and yes, you guessed it – God. Wanda then suggested that I probably should add myself to the list, which I thought was a really good idea.

Then she wanted to know who I thought I could tackle first in this difficult task of forgiveness. I decided on Mary. She had me share why Mary had been included on my list. Why did I need to forgive her? We had an excellent discussion. Then we prayed, and I felt in my heart that I did forgive Mary.

Boogers…she then told me my assignment for this week was to go to Mary, tell her how I had been feeling towards her, and then tell her: "I forgive you, and I want to restore our friendship." Shoot! Can't I just say it in my mind? Is that not good enough? No? OK…I promise I will call her this week. (Maybe she will be on vacation…I hope).

AUGUST 16, 1986 - FORGIVING MARY

Yesterday, I called Mary and asked her if I could come and visit her today. I just came back from that visit. It went better than I expected, and I believe it had to do with this prayer that I prayed on the way to her house: "Lord, it is hard not to be hurt by someone I love so dearly, the way Mary hurt me. Especially when she was someone I really hoped would be a support to me through all of this. Please help me to be honest in a way that will not hurt Mary and will restore our precious friendship. Thank You, Jesus."

The first thing I brought up was her reaction when I first told her I was pregnant. Instead of being loving and compassionate, she jumped on me for "…being old enough to know that if I was having sex, I should have known to use birth control." Which we had done…and I still got pregnant. The next thing I brought up was that when I told her I was not terminating the pregnancy, she told me I should not keep it. She encouraged me to give up the baby for adoption, which made me feel like she did not think I was a good mother.

Mary explained that her reaction to my news brought back some things in her past where she was unfairly judged by people she loved. I will not go into detail, because that is her story to tell.

She also said that her suggestion that I give up the child for adoption was because she had seen how much I had struggled before as a single parent. She did not want that for me again. She said it was because she loved me that she suggested adoption.

With tears falling, I also told her how much it hurt me when I told her that day at church about the graveside service we had for Angela, and she asked me, "Why did you have a funeral for a miscarriage?"

I then explained to her that the hospital required that any child born after 20 weeks was the responsibility of the parents. They had to do something with the body, whether by cremation or burial. I also told her Angela was not considered a "miscarriage." She was born alive, lived for 14 hours, and was considered a "premature birth", one at 23-weeks gestational age.

Mary was surprised about that, and she apologized for the way she had reacted to my pregnancy, and the things she had said along the way. She was sorry that she had not been the support I needed during my pregnancy and my loss of Angela.

I told her I had already forgiven her, and I asked if she would forgive me for my resentment towards her the last few months. I told her how important her friendship meant to me, and how much I wanted that friendship to be restored.

She offered her forgiveness to me, and we cried together, hugged, and told each other, "I love you." It was one of the best birthday presents I had ever received. Yes, today is my 39th birthday.

AUGUST 30,1986

I was supposed to have another counseling appointment on the 28th and I was going to report on my visit to Mary, and then discuss the next person on my list, my boyfriend. Instead, I ended up having an emergency appendectomy that day.

"Really, Lord? Why now? I am just beginning to feel better about my life. I do not understand!"

Not what I needed. So now I am off work for the next few weeks. Now I won't be seeing Wanda again until October.

SEPTEMBER 29, 1986

Today was my first day back at work. Because I work in Orthopedics, and a lot of lifting patients is involved, most of September was spent in recovery from my appendectomy. My sick leave ran out on September 8th, so I am living on trust right now…trust in the Lord, my Provider. It is a good thing I have learned to be frugal…something I had to do before I became a nurse. It is also a good thing I worked those extra shifts in July and August. It will be nice to get a paycheck again.

I was also busy getting the kids ready for the new school year. Thankfully, I had enough money to buy them some new clothes and their school supplies. So, we were all set when school started on the 8th.

I did have some exciting things happen in September, but I want to wait to tell you about that a little bit later.

OCTOBER 3, 1986 - FORGIVING HARLAND

Today was my first counseling appointment since I had my appendectomy. It was good to see Wanda again. I was excited to tell her about my time with Mary. She was delighted that God restored that special friendship by my willingness to forgive her and to ask for her forgiveness.

After my time with Mary, and when I was recovering from my appendectomy, I wrote down a few thoughts about forgiving my ex-boyfriend, Harland. They were things I needed to deal with and wanted to share with Wanda. This is what I had written and then read to Wanda today:

"My ex-boyfriend is next on my list of people I need to forgive. Although things went well when I talked with Mary, I really am not looking forward to seeing him, especially since we have not spoken since the phone call I made to tell him Angela had died…oh, I also called to tell him about when her graveside service was. Any communication we had after that was done by snail-mail. One thing he was good about was to fulfill his offer to pay for half of my medical costs related to Angela. He also ended up paying for half of Angela's burial costs, even though he chose not to come to her gravesite memorial service.

Yes, I definitely had some hurt feelings, resentments, and anger that I needed to deal with. I also remembered that he told me he would be married by now. So, as I prayed about it, I asked God to help me let go of my resentment and anger towards Harland. Especially those hurt feelings that were weighing me down. Yes, I need to forgive Harland."

Then I told Wanda "The rest of the story" …

God answered my prayers in a surprising way. Out of the blue in early September, Harland called me to see how I was doing. I could not believe how my heart raced when I heard his voice. I hated that he still had any power over me like that. We did not talk very long, but I admitted to him that Angela's death had been hard on me. I also told him I was going to counseling to help me deal with everything. That was about all we said, other than I told him that I was recovering from my appendectomy. Neither of us mentioned his new wife.

When we hung up, a sense of peace came over me that I was not expecting. For so long, I had been feeling like I was the only one suffering because of Angela's death, while Harland was probably only feeling relief.

I thought he was carrying on with his life as though nothing had happened, yet I was still dealing with a lot of pain. I felt like I was the only one grieving for her.

But that one phone call made me realize that Angela's life and death did have an effect on him too. He had also lost a daughter. And he was still remembering her months later.

That was the reason I chose to let it all go. I made the choice to forgive him, even though I never said those exact words to him. But I think he felt it on that call because of the way I spoke to him. Maybe I should have told him in so many words. I may never know.

Anyway, after I told Wanda about Harland's phone call, I said that I truly felt that I could mark Harland off my list. I had forgiven him. Wanda and I then prayed for Harland, and I confessed to the Lord that I truly had forgiven him. Somehow, I felt much lighter.

For the rest of that session, Wanda and I talked about all my anger towards God. I listed the many reasons, number one being that He did not save Angela's life, when I knew in my heart that He could have done so. Also, I talked about how I felt that He had deserted me when I needed Him most. All those nights I had cried alone, where was He? I told her that I did not understand why Angela had to die after all the humiliation I had to face in telling my friends, my family, my work colleagues, people at church. And why did He take Angela after I got to the point when I was excited about having another child? After all, I could have chosen to abort her from the beginning, and I would not have had to deal with everything I had been through in the past several months.

First, Wanda told me that it was OK to be angry at God. He was big enough to take it! She said the Bible had many examples of people crying out to God because they did not like the circumstances they were in. She told me to read the Psalms and see what David had to say. She also gave me a small book to read before our next session. She encouraged me to take some time alone to tell God exactly why I was angry with Him.

"Pray all of your complaints to Him," she said. I reassured her that He had already heard them many, many times before from me. But she told me to do it again.

As usual, we ended the session in prayer. This time, though, I did not feel like praying so she simply prayed for me. I went home with a lot to think about. We were going to meet again in two weeks.

OCTOBER 17, 1986 - FORGIVING GOD, MY FATHER

Today was my appointment with my grief counselor, Wanda. I could not wait to share everything that had happened to me after reading the book she let me borrow. This was the day we were going to talk about my relationship with my Heavenly Father. This is the gist of what I told her:

> The night after our last session, when I was alone in bed, I poured out my heart to God and tried to justify all my reasons for being so angry at Him. My tears and my anger flowed out in equal measures, almost as though they were competing with one another. More than anything, I told God that He just did not understand. I guess I am pretty human, aren't I? Haven't we all done this, telling God He doesn't understand, when in truth, it is we who do not understand?

> Several days later, I had some time to be alone and read the book you asked me to read. It was all about the emotions Jesus must have felt when He chose to go to the cross for mankind. It began with the Passover meal, what we often refer to as "The Last Supper." It was the last meal that Jesus had with His disciples before He was arrested and then crucified.

> It was there, while they were still eating, that Jesus "...took **bread, gave thanks and broke it, and gave it to them, saying, 'This is my body, given for you; do this in remembrance of me.' In the same way, after the supper he took the cup, saying, 'This**

cup is the new covenant in my blood, which is poured out for you.'" Luke 22:19-20

Then Jesus told them that one of them would betray Him, surprising all of them but one. We know that Judas Iscariot was the one who slipped out quietly to do what he had been paid to do – to betray Jesus.

After the meal, they sung a hymn, and headed out towards the Mount of Olives, where the Garden of Gethsemane is located at its base. Gethsemane was a favorite place where Jesus went to pray. Jesus knew what was coming, and He needed the encouragement of His Father in heaven. On the way, Jesus told the disciples that they would all fall away. Peter boldly declared, **"Even if all fall away, I will not." Mark 14:29.** Jesus told Peter that before the rooster crowed again, Peter himself would disown Jesus 3 times. We know that is exactly what happened.

As I continued to read this book you loaned me, things started percolating in my brain. Jesus was betrayed by His friend, Judas. Then, by all 11 of the other disciples, who were His closest friends. Hmmm...I had felt betrayed by one of my closest friends. And by Harland, when he decided to quit seeing me four months into my pregnancy. Then of course, his quick marriage to someone else. And I readily admitted that I felt God had betrayed me too.

Then I read about the agony of Jesus, as He wrestled with what He was about to face. He cried out to the Lord that, if possible, could this cup be taken from Him? That was exactly what I felt when I first found out I was pregnant. I looked ahead and saw a future I did not want. I begged God to "take this cup from me." He answered that prayer, but not until He was ready to do it, and in His own way.

As I read about the 3 trials Jesus went through - the false accusations, the floggings, the mocking, the humiliation of being spit upon by those He was trying to save - the tears began streaming down my face. The author captured the disturbing emotions and horrific bodily torture that Jesus endured even before He was nailed to the cross. And yet, He was innocent of all sin.

Now, there is no way I would compare myself to Jesus (obviously I have sinned many times in my life) or equate what I went through during my pregnancy as to what Jesus suffered, but my brain was beginning to slowly open up to some new thoughts.

When I first found out I was pregnant, everyone who I shared with – my friends, my doctor, my children, my parents, my singing ensemble, my brothers – were all Christians. Every time I shared, it was a new humiliation for me. Why? It was because they all knew that I was a Christian, and I had sinned against God by sleeping with Harland. Sadly, admitting our sin to other Christians is hard! I do not know why it is so difficult to face the consequences of our actions, but for me, this was a very painful time for me. Very humbling…

But what I began to realize was that Jesus suffered humiliation himself, which meant that He understood my humiliation, even when I felt like He was not there for me. Another thing as I looked back, I saw that every single time I shared with someone, it was never as bad as I conjured it up in my brain to be. That right there is God's grace and the grace of those with whom I shared my secret.

Now, I know I was never flogged like Jesus was, but many, many times I had flogged myself emotionally during the pregnancy, especially after Angela died. I blamed myself, my body, and of course, God.

I kept on reading the book you loaned me, and then the author described what it was like to carry the cross after being beaten and flogged to within an inch of death. No wonder Jesus fell and could go on no longer. Again, I saw similarities to my experience. When Angela died, I had such a difficult time going on with my life. I just wanted to quit. I did not have the strength to keep walking. My life ahead of me all felt uphill, and I really was not sure how I could make it, especially during the time I felt God had deserted me. Then I remembered Jesus's words on the cross, **"My God, my God, why have you forsaken me?"** Matthew 27:46b That is exactly how I felt - that God had abandoned me when I needed Him the most!

Suddenly, my heart was rebroken when I realized that Jesus understood all I had suffered through the pregnancy and then the loss of my child. Of course, what He went through was much different than what I did, but for the first time in a long time I felt that someone knew what I had suffered. And of course, everything I suffered was a result of my own sin, whereas Jesus was without sin. But I broke down and wept because I realized I was wrong about God. He did understand me - every emotion, every heartache. He never went away; I just could not feel Him because I was so angry with Him. He never quit loving me. He never left me.

As I thought about God's love, a new revelation flowed through my brain: how could I have ever thought that God did not understand what it was like to lose a child? Of course He did! He lost His one and only Son! And He had to see all the horrible suffering that Jesus went through before the cross and during the crucifixion. And when God the Father had to turn away from Jesus, His Son, because He carried on His back all the sin of the world, did I not think that that would break a father's heart? Again, I wept as that realization emptied my heart of all anger and resentment towards God.

It was at that moment when I completely forgave God. I then confessed my sin of unforgiveness to Him, and I knew that truly I had been forgiven by Him. It changed everything in my process of healing."

As I poured out my story to Wanda about forgiving God, we both shed some much-needed tears. I told her I finally understood that God was there with me through everything, even when I could not feel Him. And that Jesus totally understood every emotion I felt. I was wrong to feel He had abandoned me.

After I shared everything, Wanda and I both decided that it was time to stop our counseling sessions, except for one more time to make sure I was truly OK. She knew that grieving a lost child takes a long time, sometimes many years. But she felt that now that I had restored my relationship with God, I could stay on the path to healing. She told me that I would never forget Angela, but each year that passed would be a little easier than the year before.

When I left, I gave her a big hug and thanked her profusely for everything she had done for me. I told her I was beginning to feel better about myself and my life than I had in a very long time.

Once I got home, I thought about everything Wanda and I talked about in our time together. I realized she was right about what forgiveness can do for your soul. All my anger had been eating at me, even making me a bitter woman. And when I finally released everything to the Lord, a huge burden was lifted off me. Losing Angela still hurt, but there was no longer the angst of anger weighing me down.

—⁂—

God's Grace and God's Glory

SUMMER, 2023

Many years have passed since my Angela Joy was born, and even more years gone by before I started writing this book. The writing itself took another nine years, as I struggled to sit down and relive this most difficult time of my life. Plus, I had many self-doubts - "Who was I to think I could write a book? Who would want to read it?" But this is the most important chapter of all, for in it you will see both God's grace and God's glory. You will see God's heart for each one of us.

As I explained in the chapter about forgiveness, I had to let go of my anger with God for not saving Angela's life. What He did instead is save mine. Let me explain…

God has a plan and a purpose for every single one of us, including me, including Angela Joy, including you. God never lets anything in our lives, both good and bad, "go to waste," so to speak. He finds purpose for it. He uses what we consider "bad" things to bring about "good" in our lives. It does not matter if our circumstances are the result of bad choices we have made, or bad choices someone else in our life has made. God will use those circumstances for good. I am the first to admit that when we are smack dab in the middle of everything, we cannot see how that could possibly be true. Why? Because our eyes see the "right here and now" and not what good the future might hold.

Yet God sees the beyond – beyond our depression, beyond our distress, beyond our devastation. He sees not only how He will be glorified; He sees ways He can use these difficult things to bless us and bless others. God's vision always surpasses ours.

So, what about the "good" things in our lives? What is God's perspective on them? Personally, I have found that those things we see as "good," God sees as "preparation" – preparation for everything else God has planned for our lives where He wants to bless us. But we must be willing to walk by faith where He leads. God always gives us a choice. Which path will we take? Will we be willing to take the next step, even when we do not know where it will lead us?

Perhaps you may not understand what I have said about God using the "bad" in our lives to bring about "good." Let me share a little more about how God did just that in my life.

First, about a month after Angela died, I ran into my best friend from nursing school and her husband, Dave. Chris and I had lost touch with one another because we both worked at the hospital but in entirely different units. Plus, I was a single mother of two, working part time, and she worked full time and had no children. Chris and Dave told me they had been trying to get pregnant but had not had any luck.

Chris worked with premature babies in the NICU (Neonatal ICU), so I ended up sharing my story about losing Angela at 23 weeks. She reassured me that there was nothing that could have been done to save her. She and Dave were both very sympathetic.

Less than six months later, I got a call from Dave, telling me that Chris was 23-weeks pregnant, but their little girl had died in utero. She and Dave were at the hospital, where Chris was being induced so her body would birth the dead baby. Then he said, "What do we do? What did you do?"

I was able to share with him about burying Angela in the cemetery in BabyLand and having a graveside service for her. I also told him things I wished I had done, such as taking some pictures of me holding her, and of the child herself.

Sadly, several months later they lost a full-term baby because of a serious heart defect. Now, they have two little girls buried near Angela. That was the first time God would use me to help someone else to live through their devastation. He used my "bad" to help my friends through their "bad," which was eventually "good" for all of us.

The August after Angela was born, I was still going to counseling every other week, but ready to wrap it up. By then, I had worked through my forgiveness of others, yet I still had not truly forgiven myself. That would take many more years. But I was definitely healing; I was beginning to see a little light in the darkness.

As I said earlier, in late August, I unexpectedly had to have my appendix out. At the time, I was working every other weekend at the hospital, and a couple of days during the week. Because I had to take several weeks to recover and had not built up a lot of sick leave, I was worried about being off work again. To me, this was something "bad" in my life. But God... what did God do with this?

It turned out that the weekend I normally would have been working, one of my friends from volleyball was having a party for us – a cookout at his house. If I had not had my appendix out, I would have been working. And who did I end up talking to most of the party? A man who had been coming to volleyball off and on, usually brought by one of the regular girls. But she was in Europe for a few weeks, and he came to the party on his own.

We talked for quite a while, and he seemed very nice. Yet I knew I certainly was not wanting, nor ready, for another relationship. But I do remember going home and writing his name down so I would not forget it - Pete Banning. Little did I know that seven months later that would be MY last name. It has been for the last 36 years now. Tell me God did not orchestrate that! "Bad" to "good" – "very good," in fact.

Pete and I got married a week after the one-year anniversary of Angela's death. To show you what kind of man God brought me, I want to share a note he gave me on that first anniversary of her death:

March 15, 1987

My dearest Renée,

It's really hard for me to know how to comfort you as you remember Angela today. I am truly sorry that you had to experience such a loss. I will never know such motherly grief.

What I can do, however, is accentuate the good that has come into your life – partially as a result of your loss. I honestly believe that God has planned all of our lives and that His hand was at work preparing us for each other. Perhaps your experience with Angela helped you to be ready to love me and to make a commitment to me.

From my perspective, the way you handled your pregnancy – first, your refusal to terminate it; second, your strength in dealing with others' reactions; and third, your handling of your grief – is a very important component of building my love for you. You are a strong, capable, and extremely loving woman. You have made me very happy, and I expect to make you very happy as we spend the rest of our lives together.

I love you, Pete

I also want to share the note my sweet 10-yr old son wrote me that day:

Dear Super Mom,

I know today is a sad day for you, Amy, and I.
Thank you for giving me the seventy dollars too.
I want you to feel happy today. Amy and I are sad
too. Thank you for making me to stand a chance to
live in this world. I'm very happy for Pete and you
getting married. I love you both very much.

Love, Andrew

(I honestly cannot remember what the $70 was all about, but what I remember is his heart.) With God's grace and the love of my family, I made it through that painful day.

Two years after Pete and I married, he got a job in North Carolina, so the six of us (counting two cats) moved clear across the country, 3000 miles from home. I felt bad about not being able to visit Angela's grave to place flowers on it, but my friend Chris said that every time she placed flowers on her two daughters' graves, she would bring enough for Angela's grave too. That has comforted me over the years, knowing Angela has not been forgotten, especially on her birthday.

After we moved, I had planned to wait six months before going back to work so I could get everybody settled into our new home. Instead, six months later, I had my 3rd back surgery, which I saw as a "bad" thing of course. All those years working in Orthopedics did not do my back any good. After recovering, I still planned on working at the hospital, but my surgeon decided I had to have a weight restriction of 15 pounds. What? How many patients weighed 15 pounds or less?

When I went to the nurse recruiter at the hospital, I had to tell her about my weight restriction. Guess where they needed help? The Neonatal Intermediate Care Unit, where they took care of premature babies. Eventually, I also trained and worked in the NICU, the Neonatal Intensive Care Unit, where the babies were even smaller.

I will never forget the first time I saw a 23-week-old baby there. So very, very tiny! My heart stopped for a minute as the memories came rushing back. I felt my legs about to give under me, and I was very thankful she was not my patient that day. Because of medical advances since Angela was born, including a drug that helps develop the lungs, and another that makes them function better (Surfactant), that child had a chance for survival. I finally realized Angela did not.

It took me years of working there before I finally could let go of the guilt I felt because we had not done more for Angela. As I understood more about premature babies and looked back to the year 1986, I realized that there just was not the medical advancement at that time to give Angela a chance of survival.

As hard as it was to be around premature babies, God was able to use me to comfort others who had lost a child. I had deep compassion and empathy for those parents, and could sincerely cry along with them and for them. Sometimes, I would have to go to the break room, just so I could "get it together" again. Luckily, God blessed me during those years, and I only had one of my own patients die while I was caring for them. He was a little boy who had a terminal condition he could not survive. His parents did not want to be there when he died, so I had the privilege of holding him as he passed, something I was not able to do for Angela.

I worked in the NIU/NICU for the next 14 years, until my 5th back surgery. My back could no longer take working 12-hour shifts, so I retired from nursing, and instead had more free time to spend with our first two granddaughters who lived here. And later, free time to visit our other three grandchildren who lived away. This was definitely God using the "bad" (five back surgeries) for something that was an extremely "good" thing!

In the year 2000, I was asked to be the Teaching Director for the local Community Bible Study, (CBS) an international, non-denominational Bible study that I had been attending ever since we moved to North Carolina in 1989. I did not feel worthy to be the teacher, nor did I like speaking in front of people...my worst fear, in fact. But after much prayer and soul-searching, I felt God was asking me to say "Yes" to this opportunity.

From the beginning, I decided I would be "real" – truly honest about my life. I was not going to pretend I had always been "the perfect Christian." I promised God I would be willing to speak about my divorce – and even about Angela – if He asked me to. If I could not share how Jesus walked with me throughout my life – the good, the bad, and the ugly – why else did I have to go through it all? That was a question I asked myself – and God - for years.

Yes, my life had not gone the way I expected it to or hoped for: (divorce, losing Angela). Why did I have to go through those difficult things? One day, God answered that question through His Word, the Holy Bible. I came upon a Scripture I had read many times before, but this time the words struck me in a new way. Now I consider them my "Life Verses" – my purpose for living.

"Praise be to the God and Father of our Lord Jesus Christ, the Father of compassion and the God of all comfort, who comforts us in all our troubles, so that we can comfort those in any trouble with the comfort we ourselves have received from God." 2 Corinthians 1:3-4.

God was giving me an opportunity to encourage and bless other women who might be experiencing the same things I had experienced. And so, I said "Yes."

In the summer of 2001, one of the young ladies who attended CBS called, and asked me if I would be willing to mentor her. She said she wanted to share something with me. Honestly, I did not know the first thing about being a mentor, and again, I did not feel worthy. Yet, when I prayed about it, I felt like God wanted me to say "Yes" to her.

So, I did. What I did not know from the beginning was that I needed this relationship just as much as she did. Through it, both of us would experience healing.

We met once a week for most of the summer. The very first week, she shared with me that when she was in college, she had had an abortion. She had never told anyone except for the father of the baby, with whom she had no further contact. She said she had struggled for years with guilt about what she had done. She was a strong Christian, and knew that Jesus had forgiven her, but she could not seem to forgive herself.

After many tears (both hers and mine), and hugs of comfort, God told me I needed to share my story about Angela with her. It was hard, because it was something I was still ashamed of myself, so I rarely shared it with anyone. (As you know, I had told Pete the whole story before he and I had married, but seldom did I share with anyone else.) Was I truly ready to share my own secrets with this sweet, beautiful young lady? Would she no longer want me to be her mentor?

Both of us received comfort, not condemnation that day. Instead, we both experienced God's love and grace in a new, much deeper way. We also felt that same love and grace from each other.

We met the rest of the summer, and as we studied the Scriptures together, prayed together, cried together, and felt the love and forgiveness of Jesus together, we were both mightily blessed.

By the end of the summer, she had shared her story with both her husband and her parents, something that had burdened her for years. All of them received her with the love and grace that they themselves had felt from their Savior, Jesus. She felt both relieved and cleansed from finally sharing a secret that had weighed her down for years.

I recently learned that she has spent the last 22 years volunteering her time doing ultrasounds at Pregnancy Centers, helping women "see" their babies. This has brought her both healing and restoration. The same two verses in 2 Corinthians 1:3-4 have guided her life, as they have mine.

My experience with this dear, sweet friend, prepared me for the next time God would ask me to share my story about Angela. This time it would be to more than just one person…a lot more!

I still remember the exact time God told me to share about Angela with the whole local Community Bible Study group (over 100 ladies). It was March 2007, and that year we were studying Servants of God. We were in 2 Samuel, and we were focusing on the life of King David. The lesson that week, chapters 11-12, was when King David and Bathsheba lost their first child, conceived when Bathsheba was still married to someone else.

Of course, I still remembered that radio preacher's sermon that I mentioned earlier – the sermon that had wrung my heart to the quick. I knew that this was the time to finally share my story about Angela publicly. I was very real about it all, just as I have been very real in this book. I did not know how my precious ladies would respond, but after I finished, there was silence, and then as one, they stood up and started clapping…the only time that happened in the 14 years I taught. That day, so many ladies came forward and thanked me, some even sharing quietly about their own loss of a child or their own unexpected pregnancy. That is when I knew it was important to write this book. I felt God telling me this was what I was supposed to do. I also had many friends encourage me to do this. They believed in me. So did my husband.

So in 2014, I stepped down from being the Teaching Director at Community Bible Study so that I could fully concentrate on writing this book. Although I took many years to finish, occasionally, one of my ladies at CBS would say: "When is your book going to be finished?" or, "I'm really looking forward to reading your book."

So, I started…and then I quit…did a little more…and quit…wrote again…and quit, and finally after so many years of waiting, I think no one believed…including me…that I would ever finish the book. For several years I just gave up writing at all.

I knew that I was being disobedient to what God called me to do, yet I still felt inadequate to do the job. But this past year in Bible Study we studied Moses' and the Israelites' 40-yr journey from being enslaved in Egypt to finally reaching the Promised Land. What should have been an 11-day journey took them 40 years. Why? Two reasons: #1- they did not trust God to keep His promises, and #2- they were disobedient again and again. Needless to say, lesson after lesson convicted me. I needed to trust God to keep His promises to me, and I needed to be obedient to Him by finishing this book.

So, I started writing again, this time with a new attitude and a new determination. God has been faithful, and I am trusting the Holy Spirit to edit this book for me, as He gives me the words I should write and those I should delete. My prayer is that God will be glorified though this book and that you, my readers, would remember that Jesus is with you in your darkest hours, even when you cannot feel Him there. He knows what you are going through, because He is walking right there beside you. He will never leave or forsake you - His promise is found in Matthew 28:20: **"And lo, I am with you always, even unto the end of the world."** KJV Hold on to that scripture!

Never forget that Jesus is the Rock we can stand on, the Shepherd who protects us, the Friend we can talk with, the Savior who redeemed us, the Lord who forgives us, the Son who died for us. Jesus loves you and He loves me, now and forever more!

I would like to close with one more chapter with Angela and me sharing some final thoughts. Before I do though, I want to say that my Aunt Mildred lived to the ripe old age of 87, and fulfilled her dream of graduating from college...at age 72. And my kitty Snowflake lived to be 19 years, which is unquestionably old for a cat.

And now, Angela speaks once again.

Epilogue – One Day...Reunion!

Angela: "It has been many years now since I was born...and died...just 14 hours later. But heaven is...well, incredibly heavenly! Living with Jesus is beyond description! The beauty of His presence is overwhelming! Time does not seem to exist here, because all we feel is the awesome presence of God our Father and Christ Jesus our Lord. I do miss my mom and my sister and brother, but I know that someday we will all be together again, and this time it will be for eternity.

Mom is going to absolutely love it here because she has a passion for flowers...she is going to be so delighted when she sees the flowers here in heaven. And of course, she will be reunited with her parents, (my grandparents, Marge and Rod, who are ever so delightful...and funny, too!) And her dear friend, Elaine, who I have come to love, too! I have recently met two of Mom's other special friends – Sweet Sandy and Precious Pat. Such delights! They tell me funny stories about my mom.

Sometimes it is hard to wait until Mom gets here, but I know that one day we will be reunited. Meanwhile, our story is encouraging other women to keep trusting God, even in the darkest of times. Mom knows that God has a purpose for everything that happens in our lives. If we let Him, He can use every life for His glory, even a short one like mine. But now it is time for Mom to finish our story."

It has been many years since I lost Angela Joy, but she is never forgotten. She comes to mind, if even for a few seconds, every day. Her birthday is still hard for me, as I think about how old she would be if she had lived.

Losing a child is never something that you ever "get over," but the Lord has healed the worst of my pain. I have not a doubt in my mind that one day I will be reunited with my daughter, Angela Joy. It will be a glorious day of hugs, and tears of joy! Only then, God Himself will wipe the tears from my face. He promises us in Revelation 21:3-4: **"Now the dwelling of God is with men, and He will live with them. They will be His people, and God himself will be with them and be their God. He will wipe every tear from their eyes. There will be no more death or mourning or crying or pain, for the old order of things has passed away."**

Until that day when God calls me home, I wait in expectation to see my daughter again, but for now, she is Angela Joy, the "Joy of my heart!"

THE END

Acknowledgements

Writing a book is no easy task, as I found out when I started this book almost nine years ago. I had many encouragers along the way. Without them, I would still be "finishing." I want to thank them now.

Early on, friends Darlene Smith and Cheryl Lang invited me to be a part of Inspiration, INK, fellow writers who met specifically to encourage one another. Although I was only able to meet with them once, their words inspired me to keep on plugging away. I also want to thank Pam Frutiger, a dear friend whose exhortation to finish came at a time when I needed it the most. My husband, Pete Banning, always believed in me, and would not let me quit. My late parents, Rod and Marge Rogers, were also my steadfast encouragers. Unfortunately, they both passed away before I finished.

I thank my first readers/editors: close friends Alyce Powell and Dianne Wilson, my husband Pete, and my daughter, Amy Cicmanec. I also thank later readers/editors, good friends Pam Frutiger and Della Dixon. Their suggestions made this a better book. Any errors are my own.

Two other special friends listened from afar, as I read chapter after chapter over the phone to them: Vicki Smith and MaDonna Hartley-Parks. MaDonna listened to the entirety of my book, as I read day after day, stopping only when my voice gave out. Their encouragement along the way meant more than they will ever know.

My gratitude also goes to all the women in the Greenville CBS (Community Bible Study) who believed that this book was possible, and kept asking me when it was going to be finished.

I thank my granddaughter, Abigail Newton, for designing the cover illustration and for my picture on the back. It was a blessing being able to work with her.

A special thanks to my friend and my graphic designer, Stephanie Dicken. Without her, this book would never have been published. Not only did she format and design the book beautifully, she patiently walked me through the whole process with a smile on her face. She is a gem.

I want to thank all the friends and family mentioned above - and many more - for their multitude of prayers. I believe those prayers were the key to me finishing this book.

Above all, without the Lord's prodding, this book would not have been written. May He receive all the glory, and may all readers be encouraged to trust the Lord when they face their own difficult decisions, whatever they are. Only He can bring joy from grief, comfort from sorrow, "good" from "bad."

One other thing I need to say: this book was not meant to be a scientific study of God's miraculous creation of human beings. Angela's description of her development may not always be completely accurate, but that was not the point of this book. I want my readers to know that *The Child Within* is indeed a child.

www.ingramcontent.com/pod-product-compliance
Lightning Source LLC
Chambersburg PA
CBHW072348090426
42741CB00012B/2975